Grappling With God

Grappling With God

The Naked Truth about My Spiritual Life

Patrick Donohue

NOVALIS

Grappling with God: The Naked Truth about My Spiritual Life
is published by Novalis.

Cover: Nina Price

Back Cover Photo: Jewel Randolph

© 1994, Patrick Donohue

Business Office: Novalis, 49 Front St. East, 2nd Floor, Toronto,
Ontario, M5E 1B3

Editorial Office: Novalis, 223 Main Street, Ottawa, Ontario, K1S 1C4

Legal deposit: 3rd trimester, 1994
National Library of Canada
Bibliothèque nationale du Québec

Printed in Canada.

Canadian Cataloguing in Publication Data

Donohue, Patrick, 1945-

Grappling with God: the naked truth about my
spiritual life

ISBN: 2-89088-681-6

1. Spiritual life--Catholic Church.

2. Donohue, Patrick, 1945-   – Religion.   I. Title.

BV4510.2.D66 1994   248   C94-900776-5

NOVALIS

To Jane

. . . for obvious reasons

Contents

Foreword

Here's the situation:

I meditate every day, meet regularly with my faith-sharing group, read lots of books about spirituality and sometimes even manage to publish something on the subject. You might almost say I'm a holy guy.

Except for my frequent outbursts of irritability and bad temper.

After one of these rages, I blurted out, "How can I write anything about the spiritual life? At times like this, the very notion of faith seems like a farce, a horrible black joke! If people knew that I could feel this way they would never accept anything I might write about God."

My wife Jane said, "Maybe you should write about how you struggle through the bad moods."

"Shouldn't there be some secrets?" I protested.

"Not if you want to help people."

She's right. The world needs a new kind of spiritual writing—one that shows the complexity and ambiguity of the life of the Spirit in a contemporary person's soul. In spiritual writings, even in the autobiographies of the saints, you seldom get a strong sense of how complicated life can be. Spiritual writers stick to lofty principle rather than discuss their own lived experience. The odd allusion is made to personal struggles and temptations, but they flicker past like mere specks on the film. You do not get any sense of life as truly lived, with its turmoil and ambivalence.

The result of such sanitized spiritual writing? The reader who is mired in grimy realities says: "The life of the Spirit has little in common with a life as messy as mine. I am far removed from God and will never have any sense of a divine presence in my life. I will always be grovelling in the depths, glancing wistfully up at the superstars who soar above the rest of us and commune with God in the stratosphere."

Obviously, spiritual writing that induces such defeatism has a disastrous effect on the human spirit.

The following excerpts from my journals are offered in the attempt to show that the Spirit is alive and well in a person who is moody, who has an active sex life within marriage and who struggles along with the rest of the human race to make a living. I am well aware of the tremendous risk in exposing my inner life in this way. It's like stripping naked in public. Not that I'm an exhibitionist, spiritually speaking! I am doing this simply because no one else will.

The point is not that my spiritual condition is special. For all I know, dynamics of the spiritual life similar to mine can be discerned in anyone who cares about such matters. What may be unique, however, is the way in which I have shown how spirituality fits into the crazy-quilt pattern of one person's life and personality. This is what has not been shown before in spiritual writing: how the spiritual life arises from and feeds on one person's daily life in a family and in the workplace with all its ups and downs, its moodiness. Thérèse Martin (otherwise known as Saint Thérèse of Lisieux) gave us a good picture of spirituality in the routines of cloistered convent life; I am attempting to show the Spirit's workings in the life of a twentieth-century spouse and parent.

Jesus' message is that the Kingdom is among us here and now. We aren't supposed to wait for some future perfection. We have all we need of his Love. All we have to do is draw on it. But we don't. And so we have failed to transform the face of the earth as Jesus hoped we would. Without claiming any such accomplishment on my part, I'm trying to show how one person can at least try to be more open to the Spirit. The theme of these notes, then, might be summed up as "Giving God a Chance."

These thoughts are culled from my journals for the period from November 1986 to February 1990. None of them was initially intended for publication. The journals were written simply for the satisfaction of expressing some thoughts on matters of deep concern to me. Often, writing the thoughts helped to clarify them. At some point, I realized that the process was a form of prayer: through learning how I felt about things, I was discovering the life of God within me, hearing the voice of the Spirit in my heart.

I seldom looked at a passage after writing it and did not plan to read these journals in the future. Once in a while when I opened a volume, the item that fell under my eyes was one I could not remember writing. Reading it was almost like reading something written by someone else. The item frequently turned out to be interesting and—the most surprising thing—it sometimes helped me with a current problem. That made me think that these notes might help other people in their spiritual journeys.

In preparing these items for publication, I had hoped to leave them in their original form so that the reader would have a sense of perusing very private notes, written hurriedly and for personal enlightenment. My instincts as a journalist, however, prevented my unleashing such unruly writing on the public. All of the items, therefore, have been tidied up and clarified. I have retained the original spirit and intent of each item, however, even where my thoughts on a subject have changed. In a few cases, I have added footnotes to expand on the original item when it seemed necessary to do so in light of my current ideas.

The items have been grouped according to major themes in my spiritual quest. While this grouping may distort the nature of the journal somewhat, it is meant to help the reader follow the progression of thought on a certain subject. Within each subject grouping, I have presented the notes in roughly the order in which they were written—except in the last chapter, where the items are grouped into subdivisions.

From the context, it will be obvious that some of the items were written during a sabbatical year in a tiny village in the south of France. All the other items arise from daily life in Toronto or from summer holidays at the cottage.

I regret the sexist language of some of the items. It seemed to me that to correct it would be to make myself appear wiser than I was when the offending items were written. After a certain point, however, there is a concerted attempt to avoid such language in my journals.

January 1994
Toronto

1

God Within

This chapter deals with one of the key subjects in my spiritual quest—the discovery of God within me. My religion could never be truly alive and effective as long as it had to do with a God-Up-There. Catholic education, as I experienced it, emphasized deep-seated prejudice against self, as though self were essentially opposed to God. Overcoming the tendency to self-alienation instilled by such upbringing takes a long time.

This morning's passage for meditation was John 7: "If anyone thirsts, let him come to me and drink . . . of the water . . . ." The meditation wasn't going well, mainly because of a persistent cough. My thoughts were flitting from one concern to another. But, along with all the clutter, into my mind came the concept of the Spirit in me. In this context, it occurred to me that these whirling thoughts and concerns *are* me. It is not as if I have to get up above my concerns, to spurn them in order to commune with God. God is in me in all these thoughts and concerns.

Becoming more and more aware of that presence, I found myself sinking down deep to a level of my soul where it was very peaceful and Spirit-filled. It was as if, rather than trying to rise above my concerns, I had to get to that still place in the midst of them where the Spirit dwells. I had to see these concerns as manifestations of the life of God in me. In the end, the prayer period was a startling experience of the Spirit's indwelling. This apparent trivia that comprises so much of my life, I discovered, is an expression of divine life in me.

•

Is there part of me that thinks I should someday, somehow land in the perfect job, where I'm totally fulfilled, recognized and loved, where there will be no conflicts, tensions or frustrations? Yes. Through one's idealistic, almost Platonist religious training there is embedded the delusion that somehow such a plateau can be reached. Of course, one does not explicitly admit to such a belief. One always bows dutifully to the exigencies of the "real world." But I am always subconsciously longing for the ideal situation: "That is my destiny; God intends it for me." There is almost a sense that it is my due, in return for trying to be a good Christian.

Just as I write, it amazes me to see how deepseated and foolish that notion is. Look at the way some people are endlessly searching for some elusive "vocation"; others are always trying to discern some marvellous pattern that amounts to "God's will." All that seems to imply a longing to escape the messy realities, to escape to some kind of serene monastery of perfection. I am in the process of finding more and more that the quiet voice of God whispers to me in the messy realities. I find God in the very ordinary circumstances. My life's significance is not to be found in some beautifully polished role that I've carved out for myself. All the effort to convince myself that God wants some such role for me is really just an attempt to persuade myself that I deserve it.

•

In Sean Caulfield's *The Experience of Praying,*[*] I came upon a passage in which he says that, to the contemplative, all things are relevant. There is no screening out, no selectivity, in our continuous and ongoing rapport with God. This pleases me very much, because it corresponds so well to what I'm finding about the omnipresence of God. While meditating on Wisdom, Chapter 11: 21-17—"You love all things, nothing would be if you did not sustain it"—I was struck by how powerful that concept is. Either you accept it or you don't. And if you do—Wow! Your conversation with God never stops. I think that, as a result, I'm a little more peaceful and patient. This partly explains how Jane and I got through the drywall work so well together on the weekend.

•

I was wondering if I should stop making these journal notes. After all, they take a lot of time. Maybe I'd be freer and less obsessive if I'd just forget about my ideas and move on, not fussing about recording them. But it occurs to me that this writing is a form of prayer in the sense of self-discovery, and thus a discovery of God in me and in my relations with others. So this writing down of ideas has value as a religious act. As for whether I ever read them again, or whether anybody else reads them, that doesn't much matter now.

•

I have been thinking about the parenthood of God. It used to seem to me that God was the kind of benevolent parent who arranges everything somewhat as a master stage manager working behind the scenes. But maybe God is more like the supportive, encouraging parent who waits to see what you're going to do, how you're going to discover yourself, what you're going to make of yourself. Not a manipulative parent (wouldn't

---

[*]   Sean Caulfield, OCSO, (Paulist Press, 1980).

that be a travesty of free will?). I was standing at our bedroom window looking out, and I had a strong sense of God as the loving father standing by my shoulder and affirming me as a man, not a puppet or a plaything in his hands, telling me with admiration and pleasure: "You're doing well; keep it up."

•

Whence comes this sense of the love of God sustaining me from within? I suspect that it has something to do with the kind of love my parents showed me—a profound sense of my being valuable. This was closely related, either explicitly or not, to the all-embracing love of God. In other words, life-sustaining love from my parents and from God are deeply connected in me. Not that there weren't problems in terms of parental approval. I suppose no one has experienced it fully and unconditionally. But it seems obvious to me that experiencing a large measure of it has a lot to do with feeling that God is sustaining you from within. After all, the expression of our parents' love is a very real expression of divine life among us. You wonder about people who haven't had enough love from their parents. How do they ever come to true confidence in God? It is important that we try to show some of that love to everybody else, in case they haven't had enough of it in childhood.

•

Yesterday, at the end of a prayer period in the morning, I felt very tired and afraid that it would be hard to get through the day. So I'd have to ask for God's help. But then I thought: is this a God on high, whom I am imploring to look down and throw some crumbs my way? Or is this God within me, who is in every breath I take, every step, every move of my little finger? And the answer came: Yes! This is the God in whom I live and who sustains me. It doesn't matter that I am tired; each tiny act I can manage is an expression of the gift of life, of the presence of God in me. So anything beautiful that I see, anything delicious that I taste—it's all the presence of God expressed in my aliveness.

●

It often seems that if only things would work out better I could feel closer to God. In a moment of sexual frustration, or a moment of disappointment, or anger at the kids, or worry about money or illness, I tend to feel, "Well, I can't really love God at this point but, if things improve, I will."

How fascinating that these moments of annoyance or worry are really just moments of self-loathing, that is, a distancing of myself from myself, not from God. God is never apart, never removed. If you could recognize that, you could face the disappointment without the sense of alienation and the anger. Since God is in you, sustaining you with your own life and your love for yourself at all times, there's no reason to feel that you need to struggle up out of your lowly, unsuccessful self to meet God on some plateau where you can put on a cheery face and pretend that you're holy. I say you don't *need* to feel that way, meaning that maybe you can *learn* not to—but it seems normal enough to feel that way at times. Or is that feeling just a product of my self-alienating education—the sense instilled that I am never good enough and I really should be somebody better?

●

I hardly ever record my very black moods. By the time I get to writing about them, they've usually dissipated. Already, this seems to have happened to a large extent in this case. But, to try to recap what happened last evening:

When I arrived home, the kids were frisky and irritating. Jane gave me the very distressing report on the bathroom leak, the plumber's opinion being that we'll probably have to tear up the new wall and/or floor to replace the old pipes. Then Jane was bitchy at the kids as they got ready for baseball, leaving me to eat alone. However, I seemed to recover quickly from the shock of the bathroom business. Out walking, I was able to be "philosophical" about it, figuring the repairs would only cost a couple of thousand dollars at the most. Other people have had much greater disasters, I told myself.

My walk ended at the baseball game in the school yard where I saw both kids do quite well, which was very pleasant. But, as they were getting ready for bed, Michael asked about the problem with the bathroom. I was rather short with him and asked him not to discuss it. Later, as Jane was tucking him in, he asked about it again. I screamed at him to shut up. Then it hit me how disappointed I was about the bathroom, having hoped to show off the renovations for Madeleine's First Communion party.

Well, the self-hatred was very strong—mainly for screaming at Michael, but also for being so unstable, being unable to sustain the "resigned" spirit. I'd thought I was taking the bad news so nobly. I had been so very pleased with myself (and feeling a little superior to Jane in her dejection), but now I had shown myself to be as weak as anybody.

Later, I explained to Michael that it wasn't his fault that I got so angry, telling him briefly why the bathroom business was so upsetting. But downstairs with Jane, I ranted about how children make life so difficult. And then came a long tirade about how I'm trying to be adjustable, to accept life's problems, but that it's very hard. At bedtime, I finished off with an explosion about how I was sick of being me, how it was a rotten trick to put a person on the face of the earth, make him a parent, and give him such poor coping skills, how I was disgusted with my bad character, that I used to think I had a nice personality but that I'm discovering more and more that I don't, that I'm mad at myself for crabbing and complaining all the time, that we haven't had a pleasant evening in ages because of these bad moods, and so on.

It's astonishing. In these moods, God seems so far away, so absent. It's hard to understand how I can have felt such love and trust previously, and now feel such total alienation from God. This morning at prayer time, I just sat there confronting these black feelings, admitting that I did not want to pray, that it would be ludicrous to presume to. I'd thought of reading the Lilies of the Field passage in Luke's Gospel, one of the prescribed readings for the week, but couldn't face it.

But then something came to me. I think it was in the process of mulling over whether a favourite Psalm such as 139 would help. What struck me was that the moments when I can't love God are the moments when I can't love myself. It's when I loathe myself that the notion of a loving God is a farce, an affront, a myth. So this shows the depth of the union between self and God—the extent to which God is tied up in every fibre of my being. When I love myself, I love God; when I don't love myself, I don't love God. That's how close the union between self and God is. I'm not saying that self and God are identical, simply that love and acceptance of the one involves love and acceptance of the other.

Thinking about this, I was touched by grace. Something moved very deep in my soul where I never seemed to have been touched before. It seemed possible then that I could be angry about Michael's question, disappointed and sore about the bad luck with the bathroom, and yet aware of God's love towards myself working in me, I could take myself gently and lovingly in both hands, acknowledge that it's understandable and human to feel this disappointment. Trusting in God's love for me even in this broken state, I wouldn't wreak havoc on the family.

•

The process of getting in touch with God inside myself—I think of this as a new discovery. Looking back, however, I see that many beautiful and wonderful experiences of contact with the divine were actually coming from God within me. For instance, those times as a kid, when I was thrilled and uplifted by the church on a summer day: the cool marble of the communion rail on my bare knees, the glow of the vigil lights, the churchy smell, the coloured blotches on the walls from the stained glass windows; above all, the sense of being riveted by the gaze of God from the tabernacle. I used to feel as though the clouds had parted and a ray of divine light came down from heaven to shine just on me. But now I see that all those sensations of delight were from God within me ringing those chords which produced such pleasure. Similarly, when I was kneeling before a prairie sunset, or feeling the Spirit's presence in our faith-sharing group*—those too were not instances of a God from above bending down to me, but rather God within me, who knows me so well, touching strings which produce such satisfying resonance for me.

•

One of the processes that's taking place this year† is a gradual getting in touch with my true feelings. I suppose this is an expected outcome of hermitage. Maybe it's because I'm freed of so many of the conventions of conversation, the expectations of friends, the obligations of routine social intercourse and the presumptions thereof. Certain people, perhaps many, depending on their upbringing, take a long time learning to identify how they really feel as distinct from the approved attitudes. The process of discovering one's true feelings is not self-indulgent. It is a responsibility, a process of growth, of finding God in ourselves. God gave us feelings for a reason. They make us human. We're not purely thinking beings, so we can never

---

* This is the small group of people with whom Jane and I meet to reflect on Scripture and to share our awareness of the Lord's presence in our lives.

† Our sabbatical in France.

begin to meet God in our true selves unless we know our true feelings.

•

In prayer this morning, Jesus was like a stern, questioning presence. By "stern" I do not mean harsh or accusing. Maybe "stern" is too hard a word—perhaps "persistent" or "clear" or "all-seeing" would be more like it. The beauty of it is that he is not some authority from without who is taking a hard line with me and of whom I have to be afraid or resentful. Too often in the past I have knuckled under to this authority figure, only to find in the long run that I loathe trying to live up to his demands. No, this is Jesus inside me, who knows me through and through, better even than I know myself. In other words, Jesus is the true goodness in me, speaking to me of my best interests.

•

Here's a very important prayer experience. While praying the other morning in the kitchen, I got to thinking of the presence of Jesus here and now in each of us. And it suddenly occurred to me that Jesus is a different person for each of us. We all have our own interpretations of what Jesus is like. And this is to be expected— *because Jesus is the good inside each of us, speaking to us in our own way, bringing out our unique goodness and loving the sin out of us.* This explains how, for one person, Jesus is the gentle lover and for another person he is the challenging radical. He speaks to what is best in you. He *is* that goodness in you striving to find expression.

•

I have been thinking about how parents are dragged beyond themselves when raising kids. You have to put out for them far more than you ever imagined you could. (At least I do!) This raised the old religious issue: "Self versus the will of God." Many spiritual writers of the past talked about the approach to God, to holiness, as a denial of self—learning not to do your own will and to do God's instead. As though self and God were unalterably opposed. I can't accept that. But I begin to understand the concept of self-denial in a way that fits very well with my sense of personal development and good psychological and emotional health. What happens is that God causes you to grow and become more than you would be if you insisted on remaining within the narrow confines of your self as you see them. It's a process of *growth*, not *negation*. Or, it could be put this way: what you are denying is the limited self, the self that wants to close in, rather than to grow and become more connected to others and to life, and hence to God.

•

The other day I was thinking of a young woman featured in a radio documentary on spirituality. She was talking about how she loves to revel in the feeling of being alone with God, the feeling that God is looking at her and so on. It all sounded a bit silly—the fervour of a religious neophyte. But today, I thought: what's wrong with that? It is an experience of being in love with life, of finding that you're very happy to be yourself, to be alive. This is certainly a genuine experience of God speaking within you, making you feel alive and loved. The only problem is that the woman cloaks the experience in a lot of religiosity, making it seem "sublime" or "special" in an exclusive sense, rather than an ordinary, everyday experience that God wants everyone to have.

•

One night while walking in the fields, I was feeling discouraged with myself and fed up. I was thinking: there cannot be any good in me. But then I thought: *if God can be in that man who wandered around Palestine preaching to people, then I guess he can be in me*. I felt in my chest a physical identification with the man Jesus and with the divine Life in him as in me.

More and more I come to see Jesus as a man. It's almost frightening to see that what we're talking about is flesh and blood, bones, humours, gases, and all that. He did not provide us with an escape from our human limitations. On the contrary, he came to show that Divinity is here in this human nature. Christianity is not an escape from any of this into a perfected existence.

•

On Christmas eve, I was crestfallen and disappointed. My stomach wasn't well after the bus trip and I was very tired after a poor night and an early rising. But when I had time to pray for a minute, I thought about what it means to pray to God within you for help in dealing with such problems. You're not appealing in a mealy-mouthed way to some god outside. You dig down deep into yourself where you discover that you have the strength to face this problem as you want to— as a man with his feet on the earth. You accept the disappointment, you acknowledge that it hurts, but you have the strength not to inflict your hurt on other people, thereby making matters worse for them.

Knowing that God's life is in you, you can accept life as it comes, let it flow through you, taste it to the full, feel its disappointments as well as its pleasures. Rooted in God, you want to meet life in a way that promotes all that is good about being human. In this spirit, you can grow through it all in a way that will bring you closer to others, instead of distancing you from them.

•

In prayer the other morning, I had a deep sense of the reality of God within me. Everything I do is an expression of God's life. Then what does this mean morally? It seems that, as long as I am in touch with my true inner life, I can do nothing but good. What an amazing notion! It seems preposterous, and yet I feel that it is fundamentally very true. It doesn't mean that I'm rushing around performing virtuous acts in a self-congratulatory way. It means simply that, in any given situation, the desire to do what is good flows naturally if I let it. The instinct for the good rises to the top, so to speak. The resulting action is natural, spontaneous, unforced.

Rather than seeing the good life (in the moral sense) as a constraint imposed on me, or a code adopted because it's approved by other people, I am quite confident of the voice of God within speaking the truth of each situation to me. There is no beating my head against the wall in the effort to try to figure out what "the boss" wants. Rather, there is a delightful recognition that the sense of the good, the desire for it, is essentially God in me—it has been a part of me all along.

Mind you, I'm not saying that I always choose what is best or that it is always perfectly clear to me what is the good choice to make. Sometimes it takes a while for the voice of God to come through clearly. Education and upbringing that alienated me from myself can make it hard to trust that the Spirit speaks within me. But it is becoming clearer that God within me has always wanted to choose the good and can do so more easily and spontaneously once I realize this urge is part of myself.

2

Other People

The main thrust of the notes in this section is the slow and gradual discovery of my connection in God to everyone else. I used to feel that holiness was just a question of God and me. Belatedly, I am learning that it isn't so. Discovering God within myself is only part of the story. The experience of knowing God acquires a rich new dimension when I encounter God in other people.

The other night at our group meeting, one of the guys referred to Jesus as an "ordinary Joe." Suddenly, Jesus' ordinariness hit me very forcefully. I really did see him as an ordinary guy—say, the postman. One of the texts we were discussing that night was John 14, where Philip asks to see the Father and Jesus says, "If you have seen me you have seen the Father." I imagined a postman sitting there saying that. He is saying, "Look, you can see me. See the divine spark in me. You see me trying to love my fellow human beings. Well, that is as close as you're going to come to seeing God: seeing the divine spark in your brother."

Admittedly the text goes on to talk about rather extraordinary accomplishments of Jesus, his miracles, but Jesus speaks of them in a rather slighting way, as if they're not a very important basis for believing in him—certainly not the main one. If you're too obtuse to see the real one—his personifying the divine spark in the common man—then you can look at the miracles.

•

Sometimes I'll be looking at some slob on the subway and it will suddenly occur to me: he wants the same things I want—the pleasures of sex, food, drink, a comfortable home, security, love, recognition, acceptance! And I am suddenly aware of the presence of God in our shared humanity; this is the life he has given us. This awareness must be the movement of grace, because it comes so seldom and so suddenly; yet it makes an enormous difference.

I tend to think I am the only one who has trouble accepting other people this way—seeing and loving in them the humanity we share. I find myself deficient in comparison to people like Pope John XXIII who is supposed to have loved everyone he met. Yet the people in our group say my trouble loving other people is pretty common.

•

When I use the word "love" in this context, it means something quite different from what I used to think Christian love of others meant. I used to think that it meant a heated-up enthusiasm for other people, combined with a self-flagellating determination to do them good. But now I see it as a laid-back, humorous acceptance of the foibles and weaknesses of others and a forgiveness of them and of myself for the inevitable irritations and conflicts between us. That feels a lot more like being in the presence of God than the conscientious striving to love them does. Not to say that the laid-back acceptance is any easier!

•

Lately, I've been increasingly aware of the vulnerability of human life, the tremendous weakness of the human body, the fact that it can so easily be destroyed—and, in fact, is being destroyed in minute ways every day. We humans are such pathetic creatures. This realization helps me to be tolerant of and patient towards other people. We get carried away with our own importance and forget that we're really just glorified animals with corruptible flesh, who live only a very short time. If we remembered that, we'd be much more accepting of each other and kinder—living in a comradely way (as opposed to that patronizing way which I used to think was the gist of Christian charity). I can love even the most bothersome slobs on the subway if I stop and think of them this way.

•

A realization that is coming through to me a lot lately is that I simply cannot accept the humanness of people. The hardest thing is for me to accept that people, including me, are not perfect and were *not meant to be perfect*. Getting angry, screwing up, and so on are simply part of being human and are to be expected.

•

Last Sunday at church, I was mad at everybody—cantor, celebrant, preacher, and congregation—my usual resentful, carping mood at the beginning of Mass. But then I started thinking about my visit to L. dying in hospital. At the approach of death, her need to control people yielded to gratefulness for little kindnesses such as a glass of water, a bedpan, a change of sheets. Life in the end comes down to such simple needs. Thinking about this, my resentment towards the rest of the congregation began to melt away. I found myself feeling the connection with and the need for these kind, good people who would certainly help me in an emergency, even if they didn't do things my way. And so the cranky insistence that they sing and preach my way receded. Not that I liked the way they did it; just that my dislike ultimately wasn't very important.

   This seems to be a grace that I'm getting from L.'s illness. The message holds true, even though my subsequent visit to her showed that she'd had cranky, paranoid spells, especially at night. She was trying, though, to be patient and resigned. When I asked if she minded the fact that the nurses had turned up the bright lights, she said, "I try not to let it bother me."

•

   Sitting in the church at L.'s funeral, I had one of those intimations of heavenly peace, of grace, of the presence of God. It came with this thought: in death/eternal life, the old rivalries and contentions don't matter any more. There probably wasn't a person in the church that L. hadn't angered at some time. Yet, they were all praying for her.* It was a feeling of the goodness of the "old home town." There are lots of antipathies and feuds, along with the allegiances, but in the end there is loyalty and community love and support when you really need it.

•

   After four days of visiting relatives, I am convinced that the meaning of life is simply to try to get along with people. By this I don't mean a sort of nicey-nicey determination to smother everybody with love and good cheer. On the contrary, the secret is to let people be. To let them be themselves. To let them find themselves. To affirm them if you can, but at least to let them find their own way, even if you don't particularly like what they make of themselves. This occurred to me in the midst of all the phone calls, the coming and going, the manifestations of everybody's different whims and desires—all of which can be so tiring. Often,

---

   *   A cynic might say some of the mourners were there to dance on her grave. But it didn't seem so to me.

you find yourself listening to somebody go on about something when you feel they're on the wrong track and you're not interested anyway. Instead of condemning or criticizing, you just let them be and try to appreciate, if at all possible, what they're interested in.

So what I'm talking about is *tolerance*. It seems so simple, really a platitude: Live and let live. So why does it strike me as a revelation? Maybe because this new outlook is so very different from the lessons of my upbringing: that there was a level of perfection you were obliged to strive for, and that you could not suffer slobs who refused to reach for the same plateau.

•

While watching movies on the weekend, I started wondering whether it is only Christianity (my understanding of it) that involves a kind of "lowering" process instead of striving for greater heights. Many religions talk about reaching higher levels of being; the spiritual life is often described in terms suggesting a constant upward motion. But it seems to me the essence of true Christianity is a levelling to the point that you're in touch with your fellow human beings, that you're aware of the roots of your common humanity. Other religions express somewhat the same idea in that they talk about getting in touch with all things, sensing your oneness with the universe. But mostly they seem to talk about it as reaching a higher level. In my understanding of Christianity, it's done more by a process of *reductio*. Jesus talks about giving a cup of water, clothing, food—meeting the most basic human needs—as the most important manifestations of our connectedness in God. (Of course the seeds of this teaching are present in the Psalms and other books of the Old Testament.)

This theme occurred to me because what was fascinating in many of the movies was the uniqueness of the many characters—the drunks, the thieves, the degenerates, the kooks. I was finding them loveable. It struck me as amazing that this feeling is the essence of my religion.

•

As usual, I was in a snit about departure from the island. Having not slept long enough and having drunk too much coffee, I contributed more than ever to the tension over the packing-up process. Added to all the customary hassles was the anxiety about the rough water. I was much inclined to snap at everybody and blame my bad mood on them. But while I was washing the dishes, it occurred to me that there were plenty of good reasons to be anxious without trying to pin my problems on other people's faults. Then, I started handling the preparations for departure more smoothly, trying to deal with each problem as it came up, rather than being in such a muddle of anxieties that I lashed out at the wrong things.

And so, in the process of accepting my own bad mood, I got to thinking, yet again, that the meaning of life is to learn to accept other people's flaws and faults, their anxieties and needs—and so to love the *humanity* in them. Somehow, I picked up an absolutely wrong idea of the meaning of life when I was growing up. I thought the goal of life was to strive to be perfect and to try to get other people to do so. It amazes me that I could have picked up such a completely wrong idea. I'm inclined to blame it on the tutelage of my elders, but maybe the problem was my misinterpretation of their teaching and attitudes. How can they all have been so wrong?

There were signs, occasionally, that I was missing something. I never truly understood my father's statement to me, "One loves people for their faults." I wondered how he could say that. It seemed to me that all the people worth admiring and loving (I tended to equate the two) were just about perfect. To the extent that they lacked perfection, I tried to overlook that.

•

Jane was trying to arrange something over the phone, but came away saying that So-and-So was in a bad mood and didn't want to discuss the item. To my amazement, I found myself saying for the first time: so he's in a bad mood—well, I don't condemn him for that, I can accept his humanness. It seems to me that this is real progress in my life struggle. I think it comes to a large extent from Jane's accepting my bad moods. This helps me to learn to accept them.

•

While reading a *Globe and Mail* article about Stanley Knowles, the old MP, I was struck by a paragraph saying that his upbringing had convinced him that the central message of the Gospel is the struggle for social justice for the poor. That definitely was not the central message of the Gospel in my upbringing. The message that came through loudest and clearest to me was: moral and spiritual perfection and the need to strive for them.

So there we are. It's humbling to admit that the message of social justice isn't in my bones.* But I have to recognize who I am. Identifying the ideology that formed me is the first step to deciding what to do about it. But it would be deluding myself to think I could simply jettison it and be somebody else. It seems to me that I will always have to work with that "nature," but that doesn't mean that I have to subscribe to it wholeheartedly and blindly.

It's not that I was ever completely lacking in compassion. After all, the striving for perfection meant that you would, of course, love your fellow humans. But the self-perfection came first. The compassion (more than justice) was to be a consequence of it. That difference in priorities is what's so telling.

•

---

* But who says it isn't in my bones? Maybe it was my *education* that was lacking, not me. The education failed to bring out what was in me.

A bad mood most of the past week, largely because of flu and a cold. Spent a lot of time lying in bed, bored and depressed, not feeling like doing anything. One night it occurred to me that I was sick and tired of being Patrick Donohue. I didn't like anything about the parcel of moods and feelings that is myself. Things I had liked about myself formerly seemed out of reach now.

Which brings me to the observation that there is much about ourselves that we have absolutely no control over. Look at kids. Why does this one hate quiche? Why does that one dislike milk? These are simply traits they're born with. So much of who we are is just what we're stuck with. Given that situation, we should be much more patient with ourselves and others. We get caught up in illusions of our control over ourselves when really we are marginally less predetermined than animals. We make too much of that very slight yet significant self-consciousness that distinguishes our species. Sometimes, I step back from the feuds that our self-importance gets us into. I try to look at us from God's point of view—as the not-very-powerful creatures we really are.

•

The feeling often comes over me lately that I have to reach out to other people and ask for forgiveness and support. There are times when, in spite of my lofty notions about myself, I do not know what to do. Indeed, I do wrong. As a result, I feel more in touch with common humanity.

•

I have been intending for a long time to make a note about my increasingly catholic (small "c") world view, or what might be called my development of a broader tolerance. I often encounter points of view which irk me at first but not for long. The initial annoyance has to do with the fact that these attitudes represent earlier stages which I've cast off, or that they seem antiquated or inappropriate or whatever. But eventually I can accept them as part of the overall picture of humanity, each point of view forming a relevant piece of the huge mosaic. I find it much less necessary to insist on the dogma that seems right to me. My ideas may be the best for me but I can let the others have theirs.

Reading the J. H. G. journals, for instance,[*] I was somewhat disturbed by his tremendous happiness about the presence of the Blessed Sacrament in his cabin. I remembered feeling that kind of devotion once upon a time, but it didn't seem appropriate now. To me, the more important emphasis should be on the presence of Christ in each person. But then I thought, "Well, those feelings are fine for J. H. G. in his own time and place. I can appreciate that such devotion was helpful to him. Even if here and now somebody feels the way he did, I can accept it. They don't have to feel the way I do. Their feelings are part of the hymn that humanity sings in God."

And here's the surprising thing: because those attitudes are meaningful to those people, they can have *some* of the same meaning for me. If I respect the other person's feeling, then, by something like osmosis, the aspect of the faith that's so meaningful to that person becomes more meaningful to me. Or, at least, it takes on a shade of meaning it didn't have before.

•

In the novel *Tom Jones*, the old man of the mountain said he'd decided that a lifetime was not too much to devote solely to the worship of such a great and all-good Creator. It struck me that this was perfectly true, and that I would like to do it. The only point on which

---

[*]   *The Hermitage Journals*—the diary John Howard Griffin kept while living in Thomas Merton's hermitage and working on a biography of Merton.

I'd disagree with the old man was that he felt he had to do it in solitude and in alienation from other people, rather than through and with other people.

●

In the past, my acknowledgement of my sins against charity was based on a vague instinct that one should be kind. The people who did or did not receive kindness from me were virtual objects and thus quite separate from my all-consuming self-centredness. My mandate was simply *to deal with them*. The emphasis was on my own narcissistic cultivation of virtue, of "niceness"—not on a true awareness of God's presence in others linking them to God in me.

●

Sunday morning I was in a bad state because of the blowup the day before. It was a very black time. I was lying on the bed after breakfast, feeling that I could not cope with the human race or myself. Then I got to thinking about what Jesus went through. He experienced the worst that you can experience at the hands of other people. They killed him. Even his friends and loved ones (most of them) betrayed him. And yet, and yet . . . he did not give up on them. He experienced life at its most awful, yet he could still have hope and faith and love. Easter morning came, proving that he was right— that hatred, betrayal, pain, death are not the end. They're not what life amounts to, even though it sometimes seems to.

So I gradually began to feel that I too could continue to trust, to love. There might be only the tiniest spark of love left in me, but it would not go out. I could trust God to let it grow slowly and become warm again. And so, acknowledging the presence of this spark—not that I actually felt it in myself, but I could see how it operated in the life of Jesus—I could begin to be gentle again, to start again, to try again to establish good, loving relations when it had felt as if all were lost.

•

When I say this life is so *very* different from my expectations, what do I mean? I guess I'm thinking of having to go through such pain, such awful blackness to arrive at true love and forgiveness (of self and others). It astounds me that I don't have a readily available supply of love that I can draw on at all times. I had thought that I would always have plenty of that in reserve, that that was what life and Christianity would be like. However, not only is the process of arriving at love different from what I had expected (going through such black, tangled jungles), but the result is even more different. The love is quieter, more humble, accepting, grateful for the love of others as a gift, thankful for their lives and mine. Formerly, I'd thought of love as being puffed up with self-importance and brimming with benevolence.

•

After discovering the vandalism of our car, I wanted to shoot the guys who'd done it, or, preferably, castrate them. But I prayed the Psalms recommended for times of trouble and despair. And again I thought of what Jesus went through—the very worst that humans can dish out. And with the help of his Spirit, I thought: well, when all's said and done, you can't deal with people that way (shooting, castrating).

•

"Come unto me all you who labour and are heavily burdened and I will give you rest . . . For my yoke is easy and my burden light." While meditating on this, I thought: "Oh yeah? *Light*? Martyrdom? Persecution? Stoning? Can he be telling the truth?" But he is. The worst burdens are hate, resentment, envy and the like. He gives you the means of getting rid of them bit by bit, or, at least, of making them lighter. And as for the physical sufferings, they are not the heaviest, they're not the worst things that can happen—as long as you're not separated from his love.

•

I was very strongly moved by the way Jesus stopped and said, "Call him!" (the blind man sitting by the side of the road). When Jesus said that, the guy's heart must have leapt for joy: "So I have been heard! He has noticed me!" I have longed all my life for attention (love) from anyone and everyone. What a thrill it would be to have Jesus notice me as he did the blind man. But there have been many moments in life when he actually has touched me, met me, as the loving brother, friend, not in overtly mystical, spiritual experiences, but more importantly in the presence and loving attention of people, especially in certain situations with Jane and the children.

•

More and more lately, I've been thinking of the vulnerability of flesh and bone—the limitations of our creaturehood. We are so very much controlled by all these churnings and gushings within, these bumpings and flowings. I am both appalled and fascinated by a book with big colourful pictures of fish. That that is what we are—slimy, scaly creatures. That is how life began. (Think of sperm.) That is what we still are—creatures. Even with all our grand ideas.

So I try to step back from human strife and not take too seriously these tangles we get each other into. They're inevitable, of course. (Even fish fight.) But if we could see how our nature limits us and how we are incapable of rising much above it, we would be more patient, more tolerant of our bad moods, our bad feelings. This is how I want to think of my enemies when I pray about them in the spirit of forgiveness. They don't choose their bad moods and dislikes any more than I choose mine. One of the worst things about my education was the sense of "angelism" it instilled so deeply—

the sense that we are all perfectible. That misperception is the source of much harm. It would be better if a person could truly keep before his mind the awareness that he is an *animal*, with all the limitations that implies.

•

Yesterday we were busy with our visitors. I got through it all amazingly well. In prayer, I acknowledged that this busy-ness is life, these are people we love and care about, the life of Christ is in them. So it's not as if the interaction with these people was to be endured until I could escape back to my private world where Christ dwells in me. To be sure, I need that private world, the "inner cell" as St. Francis of Assisi called it. But it has to be integrated with the other world where I meet Christ in other people.

Perhaps this is the way it works: the Christ whom you meet in yourself in privacy is able to communicate with, to recognize, the Christ in other people. If you don't recognize him in yourself in the first place, you can't recognize him in them. In the first instance, I think the recognition is a bit more explicit. But among others, it becomes unconscious most of the time. You can't keep thinking about it. That would be ridiculous. You wouldn't truly be present to them. It becomes a way you feel without really being aware of it. In any case, yesterday the conscious awareness of this reality seemed to help steady me.

•

This morning when the kids went back to school after the week's holiday, I was feeling extremely tired, my body so draggy that I could hardly move, even though I'd had little to drink last night. Then there was the business of trying to help our visitors cope with their troubles. I kept thinking: how could this hassle occur today when I feel like I can't handle anything, can hardly tie my shoes?

After a lot of resentful feelings, I started thinking about Maurice Bellet's book *Le Dieu pervers*. He says that the fundamental thing is to love everyone as yourself, in other words, to accept, not to judge, to realize that each has a right to live, to be heard—that this life is a gift for each of us, that every breath we take is a gift. When I first read that passage, I felt a tremendous tug—a sense that it was an invitation to a truly radical conversion (that is, a conversion going through one's whole system right to the roots), a conversion that would change everything. In meditation this morning, the passage began to have more and more resonance for me and it seemed that this conversion was happening.

It was as if an enormous weight had been lifted off my shoulders. I felt so much lighter, happier, more peaceful. I thought of the many people who bug me and who are the major targets for my criticisms and resentments. Of them all I could say: It doesn't matter, they are that way because of things they have gone through. Some people seem still to be mired in the awful conflict that the daily round of aggression, competitiveness and lack of love induces in people. But they can't hurt me, at least not seriously, because I know that I am loved and accepted in the most important way—I have God's life in me, expressing itself in every breath I take. Sure, I can be frustrated temporarily by these people, but not truly thwarted in ways that really matter.

So my attitude towards these people is the greatest and strongest hope for blessings on them, the hope that God's peace and love will reach them as it has reached me. I'm very struck by the passage in Bellet in which he quotes Isaac le Syrien: "When is your heart pure? When you feel that everyone else's heart is pure, when you have no inclination to judge them—that is when your heart is pure." I can't pretend to claim that level of purity of heart, but I begin to see that it is the good in everyone that matters. Everybody wants happiness, peace, pleasure, joy—even if they've been through such awful things that their means of seeking happiness seem very misguided or even "perverted": more money, squelching their opponents, control of others, and so on. It is amazing how, when I think of different people who may have seemed crazy or messed up, it is mainly the good in them that shows when I see them with my heart. Granted, one has to guard against a pious pretence of loving everyone. But when you ask God to let you see each person in his eyes, to see that person's life as special, loveable, precious—no matter how screwed up it has become—then it's surprising how much you can begin to feel God's way towards that person.

I begin to sense that this is an enormous change flooding in on me. It is a transformation that I may be ripe for. Lately, I have resisted friendliness, laughter, camaraderie. But now I feel that I'm beginning to turn the corner. Maybe I'm being taken out of the shell of disgruntlement and selfish complaining that closed in around me. Note: Bellet talks about how *"l'abrupt"* (the sudden change, the rupture, or whatever) takes you out of yourself. You become someone you did not think possible when you were closed in on yourself.

•

It seems to me that I can set out with a *will* to love—not a clenched-teeth determination—but a quiet asking in prayer for increased love. Everyday I can *ask* God to help me love more. Jesus' words come to mind: "Seek and you shall find, ask and it shall be given to you." Nowhere else could that statement be more likely to be proven true, to bear fruit, than in this pursuit.

I know that this won't be an instant transformation. And, recognizing the variability of my moods, I have to accept that this intention to love will come and go. But what makes the future look different from the past is that I have at last felt what it can be like to love everyone. Even if my goodwill towards people seems totally dissipated any given day, I still feel that I have been opened up to pray for it. And it will return. Having been once shown how it can be, there is no turning back. No matter how much the vision seems to have clouded over, life is never quite the same again.

The key, I think, is the acceptance of myself in God's love. Once this has happened, it is so much easier to love everyone. There is no reason not to. You want everyone to be as at peace with themselves as you are.

•

Maybe this sudden feeling of benevolence towards the human race has a lot to do with the fact that everybody is out of the house today. I have had a quiet afternoon with beautiful piano music on the radio, a nice tea and Jane's praline cake and the Chantilly buns. She bought the buns at the bakery today because I was grumpy about not getting any yesterday.

•

The question is: can this greater love for people co-exist with the irritability that still plagues me? For instance, Friday my good mood was temporarily shattered by a phone call at tea. A very bad connection necessitated a lot of yelling. It made me feel undignified and ridiculous.

Apparently, benevolence must co-exist with moodiness if there is any integrity to my person. Let's face it, the irritability seems ineradicable. Does that mean that the love and good will are mere self-delusion, posturing? Not necessarily. In any case, I can pray that the irritability be gradually reduced. What's the good of loving people if they irritate you so much that you make them miserable? They'd have to be very faithful and trusting to see through the irascibility.

Still, there may be nothing wrong with being reminded that I have a bad temper, that I cannot always wish myself into a happy, kind state. Think of Thérèse Martin. At the end of her life, she was glad to be shown that she still needed Jesus' help to be patient when she was annoyed. This problem with irritability might be an inducement to humility (understood as knowing and accepting the truth about yourself). Without the irritability, I might get carried away by my own feelings of saintly benevolence towards the human race. I might forget how difficult it is without grace. I might start to take my "niceness" for granted, as in the past when it was easier to be nice.

Maybe this is the way of resolving the old confusion: am I the affable, kind, agreeable person who predominated for part of my life, or am I the stubborn, temperamental, irascible type? Maybe I am both types. I can be kind, gracious, forgiving—but not by way of instinctive inclination, as it seemed when I was younger and it was easier to get along with people. Rather, this kindness and benevolence are gifts from God that I have to pray for daily.

•

Today, after all the busy-ness of hospitality, I find the Gospel passage for meditation is Matthew 25, regarding feeding the hungry, welcoming the homeless, and so on. Formerly this passage seemed boring and intolerably repetitive, especially when read in church. It was one of those lists of obligations Jesus was forcing on us—we had to dole out charity as a duty, a nuisance that would be hard to fit in with my preferred life of spirituality.

But now I see the subject in quite other terms. This is the essence of life he's talking about. These simple caring gestures show to another person that her/his life is important, valuable. They are outward signs of how deeply we are connected to each other. Without these connections, we are nothing. It is in supporting and building up the lives of each other that we experience the truly human value of life, that we begin to see the Kingdom of God among us.

Thinking of our visitors in terms of Matthew 25, I see that these gestures of welcoming them, trying to be hospitable, finding them good shelter, decent beds, good food, and all that, are all ways of saying: your life is valuable, we're glad that you are you, and that you are here with us now. This is what life is all about—extending this enjoyment of life, sharing it with each other. It helps me to see my hosting chores in this light.

•

Though overwhelmed by the hectic activity of the last few days, I realize that this involvement with people has a lot to do with the quality of one's life. These threads you spin, connecting you to people, weave the beautiful tapestry of your life as a social being. I think of Madame M. taking a glass of juice to the old lady sitting under the tree. Millions of such little acts constitute our lives as loving, social beings. But the funny thing is that I am so overwhelmed by all this activity that I can't "pray" in the usual way today—I can't concentrate, can't focus or develop any of my thoughts. At prayer time, I just lie there, exhausted, arms open, accepting: Yes, Lord, I know this is Life.

•

Feeling groggy this morning after a night of deep sleep (I'm beginning to catch up), I wasn't going to look up the New Testament passage for today's meditation. The current readings didn't promise much inspiration. However, the text for today turned out to be the anointing at Bethany. Marvellous, so sensual and immediate—I could see him sitting there with the oil running over his hair, over the parting of the hair where the scalp shows pink, the oil trickling down his temples into his beard. The perfume filling the room.

Why did she do it? I guess she felt he was a fine person who needed some recognition, who needed a fuss made over him. Maybe she loved him, even physically. She was a "fan." He accepted the pleasure, the love, the attention.

What he says is so beautiful. He's not setting up conflicting values: concern for the poor versus your own pleasure. He's saying that you should be doing stuff for the poor all the time. It should be an ongoing part of your life. But it's not just "the poor" that you should be serving; it's the sister or brother in front of you at this moment. You'll always have poor people to relate to. But you won't always have this particular individual right here and now who has these needs, this desire for love and recognition. So seize the moment, be spontaneous. Don't waste opportunities of being present to people in very real, touching ways. Don't miss these chances because you're working out some theory about a more correct action.

There may be people who would respond to these thoughts in a conscientious way: "Oh yes, he's saying that there are times when I should devote myself to my work with the poor, but there are other times when I must do something for my loved ones, my family. I must make sure that I schedule enough time to give them some attention and happiness . . . shall we say twenty percent of my spare time? Let's see now . . . which should I do today, charitable work or family activity?" But that's not the meaning of the passage at all. What he is saying is: Be loving with the person who is present to you here and now. Do what love calls for now, because life passes so quickly that you may not have the chance again.

•

Further on the anointing, I was wondering what gesture would be comparable today: drinking a toast to someone? putting a lei around their neck? giving a massage or a neck rub? It's hard to think of a gesture today that has the anointing's connotations of sensuality and pampering, a pampering which was called for in those hard physical conditions. At any rate, I started thinking about things people do for each other: N. phoning us, people giving us flowers and candies for the kids . . . . It struck me forcibly that all these things—these gestures of caring, showing that we consider each other's needs important—are expressions of the divine life in us.

These are meetings with Jesus in that they are recognitions of the value of each human life.

•

When I said that these gestures were signs that we consider the life and needs of the other person important, it struck me that this is a new way of looking at "charity" for me. Formerly, I tended to think of such gestures mainly as attempts to make others think well of me—perhaps because there was so much emphasis in my upbringing on behaving well in order to be seen as well-bred. There was little genuine concern for the other person.* But it seems as if a subtle change of perspective has taken place.

•

Yesterday in meditation, I was thinking about the glowing eyes of our kids—their shining good health and their vitality. How precious they are; yet we hold their lives in our hands. Their lives could so easily be destroyed, even unwittingly. And, while walking in the evening, it occurred to me that my parents once held my life in their hands in the same way. It could have been snuffed out at any time (literally or spiritually), but it wasn't. They sustained my life, helped to build it up, encouraged it. And so did other people—relatives, friends, neighbours.

I began to think of the thousands of little ways in which we sustain and encourage the lives of each other. I'm not thinking of overt acts of "charity," but of the many supportive human interactions that we often take for granted: stopping to say hello, having a chat, shaking a hand, sharing a drink or a coffee, inviting some-

---

* Maybe this is an exaggeration. There was concern for the other person: a rather mushy, sentimental desire for the other person to feel nice; often a kind of pity or condescension. Not a complete lack of feeling, but still a long way from the kind of affirming, liberating presence to others that I now see as the essence of charity.

one to a party. All these things are necessary if a person is to feel loved and accepted in the most basic ways. These are all expressions of the simplest kind of love and acceptance. This is the expression of divine life in us.

But many people don't see that. They can be very decent and kind and yet see no connection between this behaviour and any theory about God. They feel no need to posit God's existence. And yet, they are proving the existence of God among us. Since our life is an expression of God's life, the things that support our life are expressions of the presence of God in our lives. Perhaps people who don't see this have been put off by too many references to God as "out there," "up there," somewhere quite remote, distanced from human life. It is very comforting when the veil is suddenly lifted for a moment and you see the very obvious presence of God in the many, many little things which you took for granted, but which have helped you to live and flourish.

•

While out walking yesterday, I was thinking of W. and his (to my way of thinking) sinful bullying of our kids. I was feeling pretty fed up with him. I am coming quite close to hating people here. I despise L.'s parents for their failure to supervise him. I think of their bizarre situation and wonder what kind of a marriage it can be. And I feel very judgmental and hateful towards all these people.

But then I think of Jesus and Peter—how Jesus accepted and loved Peter even when he knew that Peter was going to disappoint him in the worst possible way. Disappointment is the worst of my situation—my disappointment in these people whom I wanted to like, to trust, to rely on for some sense of community and support. Now I feel betrayed by them. Jesus saw all this; he saw that this is what humans are and yet he did not give up on them. He did not hate them even though the sorrow in his heart was so great that it almost crushed him. This is what it means to love, accept, understand people. This is when your Christian love either means something or it doesn't—when you can accept that these are weak human beings like yourself, no worse than you; that they *want* to do good; that they want to be likeable and well thought of, even when they have hurt you—and that therefore you don't hate them. So you wish them well; in other words, you forgive them.

•

This business of not judging people—of not thinking them worse than myself: often, lately, I am teetering between being really critical of these people ("trashy, stupid, amoral") or accepting them as just ordinary people like myself. For instance, I feel L.'s parents are very negligent. But then I think: no, they're nice people, coping as well as they can with the difficult business of parenting, trying to keep all the balls in the air, juggling all the different problems. There's no reason to assume they're any more culpable than I am. It's the same with T.'s parents. I tend to be very disapproving of their odd lifestyle. But then I think: who knows what private trouble they have and how difficult it may be for them? Perhaps they are to be congratulated (as is anyone) for the tremendous effort they make to keep it all together as well as they do. Or M.'s family with its erratic household. Or L. B.—I am generally so scornful of his leaving his wife. But then I think: who knows what misery he may have endured? He may be the victim after all. Each partner always is, to some extent. Maybe now he has found some measure of real happiness and release from his demons. Fine . . . I am happy for him. And I can hope that his wife has fared equally well.

I begin to sense the experience of the pure heart that sees all other hearts as pure. But it requires a kind of relinquishing, a kind of letting go. I have to surrender the instinct to cling to my judgments which are, "after all," more intelligent, mature, and worldly-wise than this pure heart. The way of the pure heart is beautiful, but I'm afraid of losing something of myself if I surrender to it. It is a bright, shining, warm place, but perhaps I prefer the cold mist of my own "reality" as I know it.

•

Lately, I've been working out/living through the business of forgiving the people who have annoyed me so grievously by their abuse of authority. I readily forgive them in the sense that I admit at once that their "sins" are no worse than mine. These are the kinds of mistake that we all fall into, more or less. But, because of the pain these people have caused us, I cannot like them as much as formerly. I am avoiding them as much as possible. In the past I would try to wipe away all memory of someone's wrongdoing. I would try to feel that all was well again, that I could like the other as much as ever, that there was no serious difference between us. But now I cannot feel this light-hearted kindness towards them. Jane, however, says she doesn't feel any residue of resentment. So I wonder if I am right.

But I suppose it's not a question of being right or wrong. Given that we're dealing with feelings here, it's just something I have to live through. It's a perennial problem: forgive and/or forget? Do you trust this person as much now? Can you keep giving that person a fresh start? I suppose that, ideally, you wipe the slate clean every time. But obviously you can't always do so. You just have to be patient with your feelings. Don't dig in your heels. Allow your feelings to change. I did shake hands with T. and said good-bye and thanks. And I've talked a little with S. So I guess things are slowly working out.[*]

---

[*] But didn't Jesus forgive and forget—cf. Peter? Jesus loved him as much as ever, even knowing about the betrayal beforehand. So this is the difference between Jesus and me!

•

The other night I was listening to a radio broadcast of a concert featuring a Haydn Quartet, but somebody coughing in the audience kept interrupting my concentration. The cough became increasingly disquieting. What a vivid and immediate demonstration of how physical we are and how limited by our material being. This person (I and/or the cougher) wants to enjoy this sublime experience, yet there's this nagging cough, just a reflex physical reaction that can't be controlled. It's threatening to ruin the great spiritual experience. It seems to me that you cannot order the person out in great rage and indignation. You have to try to be patient with the cougher and with yourself. You have to accept the limitations of our physical nature and try to deal with them compassionately. It would be hard for me to do that, though, if I had paid fifty dollars for a seat next to the cougher.

•

Have had some awful experiences with people lately. One in particular was devastating. It may, to some slight extent, have been my fault. On the whole, though, it was like a bolt of bad luck that strikes for no particular reason—like witnessing a horrible car accident and having to deal with all the trauma of it. In the aftermath, I simply have to be patient with myself and try to recover: trying not to think about it too much, while not repressing it. In fact, it cheered me up a lot when I saw a T-shirt in a store window bearing the legend, "Shit Happens." That about sums it up.

In the recovery period, I'm trying to think about nice people, friends. A renewed effort to be kind and gentle helps a lot. I turned to the crucifixion in prayer this morning. I try to do that more often when shocked by the horror of life, the (apparent) malice of people. It helps to be reminded that Jesus saw the worst of it, yet didn't give up. I'm much struck by the "good thief"— his spontaneous, courageous recognition of Jesus' goodness, his daring to go against the crowd, to speak his truth in the face of the hostile mob. His act shows that even in the worst situations human goodness can come to the surface.

•

Sunday at noon, there was a terrific crash down from my previous good mood. Due to various hassles with the children, we ended up heading for church quite late. I was in agonies of anger and frustration. Why? Perhaps too many late nights, drowsy mornings, with an on-and-off kind of sleep. Then, too, there was the wine Saturday night. In my foul mood on the way to church, I wanted to turn around and go home.

The first thing that changed my mood was the sight of that fat, grumpy lady with the flower-pot hat, her white gloves and all, passing on her way home from the earlier Mass. The sour look on her face reminded me of the time she was grouchy with our kids. How alienated and dotty she must be. I was reminded of how Jesus spotted the odd man out—the little person who was suffering. So I felt a movement of compassion: there are people with much greater misery than mine, even if they've lost sight of how horrible their situation is.

•

We think of the birds and animals as being very free. But they're not. They spend most of their lives looking for food or trying to keep warm and sheltered. We're a little better off than they are, so maybe we have a bit more freedom of choice. But not all that much.

We are such pathetic, weak creatures. Sure, we rise to the sublime sometimes, we have accomplished some pretty impressive things (impressive in our opinion, at any rate), but ultimately we're limited by our mortality, our corruptibility, the actions of our bowels, the pumping of our heart and lungs, peeing. We can't rise above all this very much, especially as we age. In the end, that's all there is—this physical body and the process of its breakdown. It becomes almost our only concern.

So we must be compassionate towards each other. That is why the true meaning of life is not in the spectacular accomplishments, but in the simple kindnesses, the love and tenderness. That is where the spirit and the physical meet in a way that is accessible to anybody. You don't need to be a great artist, a great explorer or builder, to touch the deepest meaning of life in this way.

•

[On the ski holiday] . . . All that expensive clothing and equipment on display! We humans are desperate to find some way to enjoy ourselves. Look at the tremendous amount of effort and money we spend trying to do it. Our search for meaning and joy is positively frantic.

Yet I didn't feel condescending towards the other holidayers. I felt very much one of the crowd. While I may have an inkling of where the answer lies (maybe the others do too), I have exactly the same struggles and doubts and frustrations. Amazingly, this feeling of compassion lasted through most of the week to a greater or lesser degree. I first noticed it on the train trip to the mountains. A harried, neurotic-looking woman placed her skis so that they stuck out under the seat in front, creating a nuisance for other people. She also kept an enormous suitcase on the seat beside her, hogging the space. Not that there weren't other places for people to sit, but she was making sure that she kept two seats to herself. In spite of my tendency to feel disgust at her selfishness, I also felt a certain amount of forgiveness towards her. (Not that I was in any position to extend "forgiveness"; I guess "tolerance" is the word.) I was imagining what troubles might have led her to act so selfishly and how it must not be very pleasant, when all's said and done, to be so fussy about your own comfort above all.

•

This morning, I read Matthew 18:21-35, about for-giving your brother from your heart (the story of the unforgiving servant). The core of the message really hit me: it's not a question of performing some rite of for-giveness, some bending over and graciously conde-scending to the other, not some ritual words you force yourself to say. Rather, it's the recognition that we're all in this together, we're all constantly offending, "sin-ning against" each other—we constantly grate on each other, fail to take the loving alternative, fail to act towards the other person in a way that will help that person to grow and thrive.

So this forgiveness from the heart is a feeling of reaching out and feeling our connectedness with each other, the sense that God is among us in our relation-ships to one another. Sure, we do hurt each other, and we're aware of many shocks per day, but at heart they really barely matter because . . . it is not how we set ourselves over and against each other as offended or offending that matters, but how we find God in our relationships to each other, how we help to make his Kingdom come about by our support of each other, our encouragement, our patience, our acceptance of each other's humanness.

In this spirit, I kept thinking of Z.'s irritating com-ment to me. Was she, perhaps without realizing it, pay-ing me back for my caustic remark earlier? With this inkling of what may have been bothering her, my own resentment went away; I didn't feel any anger at all. The "hurt" seemed to melt into the more important matter of trying to be sincere and genuine and support-ive to other people.

•

A dream the other night that D. [a priest] had died. In the dream, there are about fifteen friends sitting around his plain coffin. From their remarks, I learn that he was an alcoholic. He drank himself to death, ruined his life. This comes as a great surprise to me. Everybody gives a little speech. I say that I always admired him very much, that he was a good, fine, honest, humble sort of guy—the ideal priest, very level-headed. The discovery of his alcoholism has not changed my admiration of him.

It seems that my acceptance of D. stands for my recognition of everybody's human fallibility and my acceptance of it. I am coming to terms with it.

On another level—and this occurs to me just now, while writing—I see that my admiration of D. (in reality, that is, not in the dream) is based on an idealization—the kind of wishful thinking that produces a portrait of someone as perfect. You can only do it by closing your eyes to certain realities or probabilities. If I think about the whole picture, I recall incidents when D. showed signs of being as complex and prone to confusion as any of us.

The desire to idealize certain people probably has to do with the desire to put yourself down, to revel in self-loathing. By insisting that this other person has some special gift that raises him or her above the common mass, you give yourself permission to wallow in self-contempt. You can never be as good as that person; you can only dream futilely of being so.

So I see this process of canonizing others as a refusal to accept my own humanity. It is a failure to accept that I am good, with my mixture of motives, my confusion, my tendency to mistakes. It is a denial of the fact that God works slowly in me, drawing me closer to the realization of his Kingdom in the same way that he is working in this other person's confusion and muddle. By refusing to see the other person in realistic terms, I am setting up some ideal of perfection that I long for uselessly—instead of facing the reality of God in my life here and now.

Someone might ask: Don't you admit that some people are obviously better than others? No, I don't, especially not the "obvious" part. We are all good by virtue of being created and having divine life in us, but none of us knows who is better in the sense of being more in tune with God's Kingdom. Some people show special *signs* of goodness that help us to find what is right for us. What we see as good in them can help to show us our own way. But this is far from attributing a superior goodness to those persons. For all I know, a Mother Teresa or a Jean Vanier could be a totally corrupt tyrant at heart. This was the point of Jesus' criticism of the Pharisees: we should not go around making judgments of relative goodness or badness about ourselves or anyone. They distract us from the really important fact—God's presence in each person working away slowly in the quiet reality of everyday events.

•

For old time's sake I went to Fran's Restaurant downtown for a coffee and a muffin. I used to love going there for blueberry pie served by a cheerful young guy in a red waistcoat. Now Fran's is all tarted up with mirrors and chrome. But the waitress was classic: middle-aged, hefty, blonde hair, black uniform, casual manner. In came two customers: a very old, bent crone with thin hair pulled up in a knot and a couple of beaver-like dim teeth; and a plump, hearty woman companion who explained to the management that the old girl used to like to come to Fran's but doesn't get out much now because of the cool weather. Since it was so nice out today, the younger one (about seventy years old) decided to bring the older one to lunch. The ancient one talked in a very high-pitched, sing-song voice, being very pleasant and agreeable, but not having much of a grasp of what was going on. She kept asking for scrambled eggs although her companion tried to get her something more interesting. The crone insisted amiably that a dish of scrambled eggs was all she wanted. They talked about relatives, mutual acquaintances, cemeteries and relatives' graves. The crone couldn't follow much of it very well.

Here's the exciting business world of Toronto swirling around them, and this plump lady decides to pay attention to the simple desires of her old friend. That kind of encounter is what really matters. If only I could be more involved with people at that level! I'm not exactly picturing myself a social worker or a St. Vincent de Paul Society volunteer, but I wish very much that there were some way that I could relate to people on a level of basic friendship, without all the competition and aggression.

Am I kidding myself? Would I actually be very impatient if saddled with needy old people? If I'm so high-minded, why don't I do my best always by my family and their needs? Perhaps I really am deluding myself about my ability to deal with people in an authentically loving way. Anyway, I was in touch with something very important while watching those women.

•

Standing around the train station with Michael, I was, as usual, anxious about getting good seats on the train. Ahead of us in line was a group of three women with a baby boy. Two of the women were dumpy and middle-aged. The young one was thin, with straggling blonde hair, tight slacks, high boots and lots of cheap-looking makeup. She was constantly smoking and shivering in her leather jacket. They'd been sitting behind us in the waiting room. I was irritated by their banal, slangy chatter. One of them commented that the baby was so sleepy he couldn't keep his eyes open. He had a reddish, blotchy face (there seemed to be some kind of rash on it), a patch of pale hair, bleary blue eyes, and his head was bobbing. Instead of feeling fondness for the little creature, I was feeling vaguely censorious toward his keepers: rather than cooing and fussing over the baby and blowing smoke in his face, why didn't they take proper care of him, feed him properly, clear up that rash and get him to bed on time so that he wouldn't be so tired?

I couldn't help thinking of the young woman as though she were a hooker (or a "former" one, as the newspapers often say when identifying a witness in a seamy court case). It wouldn't be going too far to say that I thought of the whole group as "trashy." Obviously, I considered myself to be much above them and, with my healthy, intelligent child, much more worthy of good seats on the train. But, in that moment, the voice of the Lord said to me, of course, that such thoughts were extremely reprehensible and hateful. I recalled one of Jesus' most basic teachings: that it isn't those of us who think highly of ourselves who will enter the Kingdom of Heaven, that it will not turn out in the end that we are the ones who are close to the Lord.

So I thought: well, how is that slutty-looking young woman (you can't deny her looks) close to the Lord? Could it be possible that she is closer to the Kingdom of God than I am? The answer came immediately: look how she loves that baby and is doing what she can to take care of him. Her life is probably infinitely harder than mine; yet she hasn't given up. It would have been easy for her to get rid of that baby, but she didn't. She is also keeping up her family ties. She is giving the baby the pleasure of grandmothers and aunts—giving them the pleasure of his presence, too. In order to see family, she puts up with the hassle of a train journey with a baby because she isn't rich enough to drive. She is doing what's important in life: she is paying attention to the human values in that baby's life in circumstances that may be very difficult for her.

Admittedly, all this stuff about her life situation is pure conjecture, but it's valid, I think, as an antidote to the superiority I was previously feeling. I felt humbled and back in touch with the reality of the Lord's presence in my life. To the extent that I saw and heard any more of the women and the baby on the train, I did not feel at all hostile or superior to them.

•

The other night I was making chocolate chip cookies with Madeleine while Jane and Michael were at karate. Unfortunately, Jane had mistakenly bought choc-mint chips instead of the regular kind. The mint was so strong that it overpowered the chocolate taste. It annoyed me so much that making the cookies felt like a waste of time. I mumbled and grumbled to myself, asking how Jane could be so careless as to ruin our cookie evening. But then the thought occurred to me: why do I think my every whim and desire has to be met perfectly? Why can't I cope with a little flaw in the arrangements? If I am looking for the meaning of life in Jane's perfect fulfilment of all my desires, no matter how trivial, then I am looking in the wrong place.

So then I started thinking about the truly meaningful and satisfying facts: that we have a comfortable, happy home, that Jane's out with our son doing something he likes and I'm home with our daughter doing something she likes. When I forget that these are the important things, that is when I get so irritated with the imperfections of the people around me. The meaning of life is not about people fitting in perfectly with my plans, even though the expectation that they should is rooted very deeply in me. So I have to ask God to open me up to the new realities, the real truths of life. What is truly meaningful, what helps me to become more human, is accepting others in a way that helps them to grow and to enjoy life in their unique ways. I have to drop my expectations and wait to see how others reveal themselves in ways I'd never have expected. This is what's truly enriching.

3

Marriage and Parenting

This section might be given the subtitle: "Barely Bearable Blessings." Married love and parenting are the greatest satisfactions of my life, but that doesn't preclude a hell of a lot of difficulty in coping with all that is involved. I'm constantly examining this paradox from various angles.

The church was beautifully decorated for Christmas. Sitting at the back, I was thinking about the seminary chapel years ago:* the airy vastness of the place, the shadowy recesses, the dimness, the flickering candles, the creaking and sighing of the old building. In the imagined scene, one of the nuns was tiptoeing around the altar on sacristy duty. I remembered the religious feeling of those days—the orderliness, the sense of purpose, of doing God's will and being close to God. And I compared all that to the (relative) chaos at home now, the tension, the squabbling during the holidays. And, of

---

* I spent five years in a seminary.

course, I felt a certain regret for the loss of the sense of well-ordered holiness of seminary days.

But in the back of my mind was the reading for our next group meeting, Luke 2, about the presentation in the temple. I was struck by a reference to their doing "whatever had to be done for the child." There is so much that "has to be done" when one is responsible for children. The duties are endless. Thinking about my life as parallel to Joseph and Mary's in this respect, I began to feel more at peace. It was as though the Spirit were giving me a very clear message: looking after these kids is the most important thing in your life right now, this is really "where it's at" for you. So I simmered right down. Everything fell into focus. I came home and felt much more patient with the children, much less anxious about fitting in all my hoped-for accomplishments.

•

Something about parenting hit me the other day. Something subtle, hard to express, yet deep and important. It has to do with the gift of life to one's children and the gift of oneself in the total context. Up till now, I have looked on my activity with the kids as a sort of duty or role, albeit one very gladly taken on. I am always trying to do right by them. But I have suddenly realized that what's important is not these various fatherly acts. What's more important is simply the gift of my whole self. I am giving them myself in ways that I could never guess, thousands of ways daily. They are picking up the stuff of life from me in ways I'm not conscious of.

So it's no use my playing at being a good father. I am what I am and they will benefit or suffer accordingly. Which is not to say that there aren't certain situations in which I must try, for their good, to do what goes against the grain for me. The point is that the real gift to them occurs at a much deeper level than the obvious bending over to help them, doing the "fatherly" thing. This realization comes, in part, from thinking about my parents and the countless ways in which they sustained my life and conveyed subliminal messages about life and how it's to be lived. So I have a new sense of relaxing and simply enjoying being with the children.

•

I sit here at work thinking about what a gift and a joy our kids are and how I want so much to show them love. Then I go home and become irritable and crotchety with them. It keeps happening. I don't show them the love I want to. I wish I could quit giving them mixed-up messages.

But then it occurs to me that this is simply what life is, this is the beauty of being with people and loving each other—you have to accept the rough spots as well as the smooth. I have to stop expecting that I can show perfect love. Only God can do that. Let God be God. I should stop trying to be God. If I could show perfect love, Jesus would be out of a job.

•

Sunday morning it was raining. Jane sent Michael off to deliver his papers alone because she didn't want to wake me. But I was awake and intended to accompany him. So I quickly donned rain gear and rushed out. He had just started delivering to the first house when I came around the corner. When he saw me, a spontaneous smile flitted across his face. It was a quick, small smile. But it was all the reward I needed, not just for getting out of bed, but for many efforts as a parent. It was one of those moments when the Spirit, in a quiet whisper, speaks to you of the meaning of life.

•

Re Caulfield's book, I was deeply struck by a passage in the last chapter:[*] "Instead of our self-conscious

---

    * Sean Caulfield, OCSO, *The Experience of Praying* (Paulist Press, 1980), pp. 81-82.

efforts to be 'good' we should allow ourselves the luxury of being loved by God. And much of his love for us will be expressed through the medium of our friends' love for us. How else could he reveal it in a way that is tangible?"

That sank in very deeply as I sat staring at the green grass. First I felt the sense of luxuriating in the love of God, being suffused with it. But then I became more aware of the subtler (but just as real and deep) sense of being sustained by the love of family, friends. This intricate network of love that I barely see keeps my life together. This is Jesus' love keeping me in existence.

I was aware of the hiddenness of it when Jane and the kids came home. Not that it wasn't great to see them; the kids were well-behaved, but problems cropped up. I had a hard time dealing with them. My irritability showed that it was, as usual, hard for me to slip back into the role of a parent/husband after a few days to myself when I could take everything at my own pace. So I had to accept that the all-important circumstances of love and nurturing prevailed, even though all I could feel was annoyance.

One day we will see how total was the love that supported us throughout life. It feels like the veil dropped for a second and let me in on a secret.

•

When I speak of discovering the network of love, the totality of Jesus' supportive love expressed through others, I'm speaking of a kind of loyalty, a constancy and fidelity (in spite of setbacks) that are not often experienced as tangible or emotional love. I emphasize this because, after writing all that stuff yesterday, I succumbed to a messy outburst at the kids in which my feeling of being loved and supported by God or people was quite lacking.

•

Not tangible, this network of love? What about meals, our house, our clothes, our toys? They're very concrete signs of God's supportive love.

•

The other day at Hart House there was a lady with her baby in a stroller having lunch on the patio. She was a tall, willowy lady, very intelligent-looking. The baby was thin and alert, with a big head, very aware eyes, not much hair. After a while, the lady took the baby (it looked like a boy, about one year old) and sat on the grass. The baby pottered all over, crawled over her, tried to stand, grabbed at her, plopped down. It was all very quiet. With the sun shining through the green grass, the dandelions glowing, it was almost idyllic.

I was nearly overcome by feelings of regret—remembering my own kids at that stage and how much I wanted to love and protect them and be patient with them, regretting now that I didn't savour that time with them enough. Regretting even more that I didn't turn out to be the constantly patient and kind parent that I wanted to be.

Fortunately, the baby began to get a bit cranky and I was reminded of the impossibility of sustaining that idyllic mood. Otherwise, my self-esteem as a parent might have been completely dashed. Later it occurred to me that there was almost something a touch phoney about the scene. The way the lady leaned her elegant body back, propped on her elbows, her face to the sun, was almost like a commercial for life insurance or diapers. She might have been playing the role of the peaceful, perfect mother.

On the other hand, she may indeed have more patience than I. But what the experience brings home to me is that, nice as those moments of peace are, life is not about being in perfect harmony all the time. Life is about struggle, conflicts, the attempts to resolve them which lead to growth. This might not surprise anyone else. It surprises me. I used to think life should be like the monk in the garden serenely contemplating the birds. Having children has shown me that it cannot be so. With children, you realize the impossibility of sustaining total peace in human nature. Before children entered my life in a big way, I thought that perfect harmony should be achievable among adults and that, when it wasn't achieved, it was probably the fault of other adults.

•

Monday night I was in a state of shock and anger about the problems with our travel plans. Jane and Michael were at soccer. I decided to leave the dishes and work in the garden. But Madeleine kept bugging me with strange, babyish prattling. So I decided to sit with her in my lap on the picnic table. We looked at clouds, talked about birds and so on. After that, she seemed much more content.

When I was tucking her into bed, she said the nicest part of the day had been our sitting together. Later, I found out that she and Jane had had a big fight about her wanting to rejoin Brownies. The Brownie group was having a party in the churchyard and she was feeling very left out. So I was really glad I had taken the few moments to sit with her. It was one of those moments when the subtle whisperings of the Spirit inspire you to do just the right thing even though you're not quite sure why.

•

I was cutting up the snapshots of Jane and me for the visa applications—six photos of each of us. The process gave me a somewhat objectified view of us: who are these two people and why are they together? It hit me that our marriage is mostly a mystery. Obviously, it meets a lot of our needs, but exactly how and why, I don't think there's any point in trying to know. The meaning of it is deep and true and strong but largely hidden in God, and I suspect that this is as it should be. We just live with the reality and let God reveal the meaning of it if and when God chooses. My reason for noting this is that, in some ways, our marriage seems not to conform to the pattern that is presumed to be the norm in books, movies and the rest of the media.

•

This morning on the way to work, I was walking down our street behind an elderly nanny with a golden-haired toddler in tow. As usual, I was struck with pangs of love and regret—thinking back to the days when our kids were that age, wishing we could have been better parents, more patient, more present, firmer, and so on. But then it occurred to me: the point is not what we did right or wrong, or what we might have done better. The point is this: we have the great gift of children.

•

Thoughts after a few days home alone—I'm becoming much more excited about the way in which Christ finds us and speaks to us in every aspect of our ordinary lives. So, ordinary family life is far preferable to me than some "religious" vocation. However, when Jane and the kids came home last night, I was struck very forcibly by how hard it is for me to get back into living with others. After just four days on my own, I am very irritable about having to adjust to their presence. It's not that anybody was doing anything particularly disruptive or objectionable. Not at all; they were just being themselves. Even so, I found that, having had a long period in which I had no one's wishes or desires to consult but my own, I was very begrudging about having to make allowances, however small, for them. I am sorry about this. I love my family enormously and yet I am not very generous about giving my time and attention to anyone but myself. All of which goes to show that I need grace to respond to the gifts of marriage and family.

•

It struck me lately that Christ is truly present in the conversation between Jane and me. Not only in the conversation but in the other kinds of exchanges and silences. Now, this seems like a truism. That Christ is present is one of the most common clichés of the theology of marriage. But I must admit that, for the first time, I am experiencing the reality of it.

How is Christ present? Well, marriage is the greatest, most sublime thing two people can undertake. It is also the most difficult and challenging, the most strewn with hazards: the union of two people, body and soul, in total love, acceptance, forgiveness and harmony. Since Jesus is the human being par excellence, the one given to us by the Father to start off the new generation of humanity, then it follows that Jesus is intensely present and involved in this most intimate and meaningful of human endeavours.

So this makes me more open to the many possibilities of our marriage. Every minute we're together, something is happening in our souls, something new is growing, being shaped and formed. And we are being led to what we are to become—a destiny much more interesting than what we have been, or what we think we are. Hence the vital, existential meaning, for me, of the old hackneyed reference to marriage as a sacrament.

•

To sum up the Georgian Bay holiday, one thing loomed large: SORE THROAT. I was pretty ill. It was hard to believe that a sore throat could wreak so much havoc. In the night, when the effect of the aspirins wore off, the pain woke me like a slap in the face. It was amazing how listless the illness made me. I lolled around, not doing anything much. Saturday, after lunch, I suddenly felt much better, although for several days it hurt when I drank anything hot or ate tomatoes.

So . . . was it a good time, that is, did I have fun? Well, if that is the question, the answer would have to be NO. But I don't think that's the question. It seems to me that the question is more along the lines of: Was the Lord with us? Did we feel his presence? And the answer is YES. It was a good family experience. The children had a good time roaming and playing with their cousins. We enjoyed the closeness to nature (saw a porcupine, mink, water snake, and other creatures). It didn't matter very much that I wasn't feeling well, because overall it was a good experience for the family. Maybe for some fathers it would be obvious that the family experience would be more important than personal comfort. That's not usually the case with me.

•

I'm experiencing a lot of frustration, anger and humiliation over not being able to give our kids effective parenting, the kind of parenting that would give me a feeling of satisfaction. But today I started reading the New Testament from the beginning and I was struck by the way Joseph and Mary's life together started off with bewildering and apparently insuperable problems. Also, I read Merton's *Contemplative Prayer*, Chapter 17, and it seemed right-on: your comforting religious props have to be knocked out from under you in order for you to realize your true nothingness and your dependence on God.

This excruciating difficulty with the kids is part of that process. You have to "Let go, and let God" lead you in ways you'd never have expected. You have to know your own anger and exasperation in order to let God's love take over. Otherwise, you'd think that your own marvellous ability to be such an efficient parent was carrying the day.

Which is not to suggest that God's love is apart from, or in opposition to, myself. God's love is in me and part of me and I act it out accordingly. It's not as if some *deus ex machina* swoops down out of the skies and performs some miracle on our kids that relegates me to the status of spectator. God within me reminds me that I can and will be loving, patient, and courageous in the face of this mess.

If, however, I forget about God within me, I am likely to get a very distorted, illusory notion about my self-sufficiency. Or, overwhelmed by troubles, I am likely to give up, angry at God for putting me in such an impossible situation. Obviously, this would be a God "out there," pulling strings like a puppeteer.

•

In spite of all my anguish the other day about the loathsome aspects of parenting, it has enriched my life beyond all expectation. When you think of how this love comes into your life, expands you and causes you to grow, in the sense of caring for these other lives and giving to them, then you cannot prefer the alternative.

•

Last night, as a result of our kids' latest trouble at school, I was stomping around bemoaning our fate. I kept asking: "Why does God do this to us? Why does God give us such problems?" Now I knew that sounded stupid, and I hated hearing such a cliché on my lips. Still, I couldn't help protesting against a kind of unfairness. Why give us the very problem that we have no idea how to handle? It is so *deeply* upsetting. It leaves us at such a loss. We can think of no solution. It feels as though God has broken a bargain. We made a deal with God that life would evolve in such and such a way, or that we'd be called upon only for certain skills, and now we're faced with something that's insoluble. The age-old cry: "Why me?"

This morning, I looked at the Merton book and read comments to the effect that God is impossible to grasp.* And I realized, of course, that that is the essence of it. We cannot look for reasons, for logic, for "fair play." We have only to know and trust that *God is with us* totally in the confusion and bewilderment. Simply to know that *God is with us*—that is all. From that it follows, I think, that all that is required of us, the only skill, or the basic one, is to be with our child, to be loving, patient and compassionate. This is much more important than "solving" the problems or handling them effectively.

•

Yesterday when praying over the parenting difficulties of the previous days, I was falling into this line of thought: I'm not really suited to parenting; I don't have a lot of the talents and aptitudes required. So then the question came: What talents are lacking? Patience? Understanding? Courage? I have demonstrated these virtues over and over again in my parenting . . . . And so it went, with virtually every important aspect of parenting.

Then it occurred to me: maybe instead of looking for my failings as a father, I should see that I am essentially a good father. And so I started thinking this way. It was amazing. It was as if Jesus was saying to me: "Come on, you're falling into the old bullshit of putting yourself down; I'm not going to let you get away with that." A bolt of healing love went through me, affirming me, making me feel strong and positive about myself. It seemed then that the inclination to claim unsuitability for parenting is just a cop-out. Sure, there's no denying that I get tired and discouraged. OK, I'm irritable and bad-tempered (sometimes). But to say that I'm not suited to parenting is just to give in to the temporary discouragement and to make too much of it. It's just an attempt to excuse myself with an exaggerated diagnosis.

---

* *Contemplative Prayer* (Image Books, 1971), p. 82.

Excuse myself for what? Well, I guess it's an excuse for not drawing any more on the reserves of patience and love. If you say, "I'm just not cut out for it," then it's like saying you can't help what happens. In other words, it's declining responsibility. And I see how awful this would be—to take the attitude of a passive, helpless spectator who has no effect on children in terms of passing on love and life.

•

At the end of the prayer period this morning, I noticed Madeleine's scuffed-up white shoes under the bed. They'd been bought for her First Communion. The once lovely white shoes are now shabby and broken down by the hours of careless pleasure. They struck me as a symbol of the enormous happiness of being a parent in the midst of all the hassles.

•

I woke up about eight a.m., got up and meditated until nine while the others slept. My thoughts ran along the lines: "God, I'm sinking, I'm losing my moorings. I'm losing the sense that the small things matter (love of family, presence to one another, tolerance . . .). In theory, I believe that these things matter most, but experience is making me fed up, impatient, intolerant, and discouraged. I'm appalled at how awful we and our friends and relatives have become . . . ."

Feeling very messed up, I was wondering how anybody in such a state could ever cope with normal life and relations, especially as a parent. But gradually, I began to feel that hope is not lost, that the ideals are still there, that the love can be rekindled. You can start again. You have to do so every day. None of this was very explicit. It was rather a general sense of slowly emerging from the morass, the sticky, complicated gloom.

And I began to want to take the kids for their much-longed-for shopping trip for toys. As I was going to Yorkdale Shopping Centre anyway, this would be a good way of saving Jane a long and laborious bus trip to a toy store.

They were very happy shopping for their toys. It was a lovely morning with the kids, a delightful experience of parenting, just when, a few hours earlier, I had seemed at an all-time low. The point is that the period of prayer helped me to get back in touch with the sources of happiness, the wellsprings of hope and faith.

•

This morning at breakfast, Madeleine asked, "Do you think heaven exists?" Whereupon Michael launched into a "science-can't-prove-it" denial of an afterlife. Jane and I didn't say very much. Partly because it was too depressing so early in the morning, but also because I didn't want to batter him with dogma. We just mumbled about the difference between science and faith. I wanted to say something like: if only you knew how much the existence of God (in my view) is tied up in the fact that you came to be conceived and born, that we spend time looking after you, that we love you and try to help you to be happy!

•

Spending all day with kids who are just being kids is not all that great. A lot of childishness is really hard for adults to put up with: the bickering, the silliness, the clumsiness, the unreasonableness, the noise. Not that they're misbehaving—just being children. But because you love them so much, because you're so committed to being a parent, you put up with a lot of it. You may even convince yourself for a time that you don't mind it. But suddenly you realize how much you do.

Still, isn't it wonderful that parents *do* put up with it? This is the mystery of life—that, for the sake of love, you can endure so much that you'd never choose to bring on yourself. For endure you must. If you constrained them to the point that there was nothing to endure, their growth would be warped. You want them to be as natural as possible, not goody-goodies. Knowing that they're loved and accepted in spite of all the bother gives them the feeling of belonging on this earth.

•

I often recall Jean Vanier's statement that forgiveness is at the heart of community life. Also, I remember the *New Yorker* short story in which an astonished young woman realized that her elderly parents were going to go on and on forgiving each other the thousands of little hurts every day . . . .

In the car with Jane, I found myself embarking on a sermon about acceptance, tolerance and forgiveness. About how I had expected to become a better person as I got older and how it is disturbing to find that it isn't so—in terms of personality, shall we say, or habits and *moods*. My temper is worse, my bad moods are more frequent. Yet, maybe (I hope) there is growth and improvement in another way: more tolerance and compassion, less judgmentalism, more humility (that is, honesty) about my limitations. Maybe these are more important qualities than sociability and manners.

My sermon went on about how people cannot really change much from their basic nature. I touched on the well-remembered debate between two friends: X who was ruefully sceptical about the prospects of people changing very much, and Y who was fervently insistent on the possibility of marked change. Over the years I've come more and more to appreciate the wisdom of X's realism—and to shun the screwed-tight eagerness of Y. In fact, I have a secret admiration for X and his wife—the way they've adjusted, the way they've obviously learned to compromise.

There is love in that process. Love that sustains and nourishes. Each partner grows enormously and becomes someone quite other than what she or he would have been without this marriage. But it is slow and gradual development; the change is not drastic.

And the love is quiet, unobtrusive. Not a blaze of glory—not, at any rate, in any of the marriages I have observed. Sometimes I have heard writers (usually celibate) describe certain married couples as sublimely united in all things. That doesn't sound like any marriage I have known. My impression is that the union of marriage, while deep and real, is often almost imperceptible.

Regarding my character flaws which are becoming more noticeable—the irritability for instance—Jane said, "I guess you just have to try to find out what it is that bugs you, and avoid it as much as possible." Apparently, she meant "you" in the third person, that is, "one", in a general sense. But it was obvious that, in saying this, she was also extending healing and forgiveness to me.

•

What I can't stand are these sudden reversals. I'm going along, thinking things are much better, and then the rug's pulled out from under me again. The constant upheaval is intolerable. I have no optimism that things will work out (even though I know intellectually that they probably will). I have no courage, no hope, no faith.

When Jane came to bed, I exploded again. One of the melodramatic things I said was, "I wasn't raised for such constant defeat." I've got over wanting to be a star in other respects, but the one area in which it's really important to do well is my relationship with the family. This is screwed up and I can't do anything about it. Another thing I said—and this was less melodramatic and closer to the truth—was: If there is a way of getting through this, a way of continuing this life and profiting from it, I don't know how. I haven't yet discovered the way. I thought we had been through the hardest parts of parenting. I thought we had come up with beliefs that sustained us. But now, none of my beliefs do me any good. There is no guiding thought that provides any consolation or support.

Exasperated, Jane didn't have much to say. She wanted me to come to bed so she could give me a back rub to relax me, but I wasn't in the mood for that. I had to go downstairs and, in a daze, flip channels on the TV. The more vapid the programs, the better. As soon as a commercial started, I simply moved on to the next station until there was another commercial, repeating the cycle many times. The force of my rage abated, but every once in a while the thought of our problems would come back with an ache.

The only feeling, apart from my pain, is the thought that I do love the family. It seems as though all that's left is love for them. Paul says that faith, hope and charity will last (1 Cor 13:13) but that love is the greatest of them. At this point, it seems to me that love is the only one that lasts.

•

It feels as though my outlook on life has fallen to pieces. How can I pick them all up and put them into some coherent order? How I can re-make my personality or my psyche? There must be some new way of approaching life that will make it less painful, or, at least, that will make the pain bearable without such desperate reactions.

The possible new approach that occurs to me is that I could be more open to what happens, that I could try not to have my sights set on specific "successes" with the children. My controlling nature is getting in the way. I have clear ideas of how children should be, and what their place should be in my life. I am not open enough to learning my parenting from their unique development and adapting my style to their needs. In other words, we as a family have to function more as an organic community. It surprises me how much, in spite of all my religious attitudinizing about the great vocation of being a father, I still fall back into a very patriarchal frame of mind. I want to set down all the rules. My own private agenda is paramount. I am not open enough to the changing needs that family life presents.

•

I have been much irritated lately by the children at tea-time. The question in my mind is: Could I take my tea alone upstairs, or go to a restaurant? But then, at our group meeting, the meditation was on the Lilies of the Field in Luke. A thought came to me about the injunction "Seek ye first the kingdom . . . ." It struck me that the Kingdom for us at this time is precisely such things as being with our kids at tea-time. This is a very valuable experience for all of us. How many kids have one parent, let alone both parents, to come home to after school? And yet the world would be much better (in my opinion) if children did come home to their parents every day.

So I decided that for the sake of the Kingdom here and now, the place to have tea is with the family. (After all, I have solitude most of the day.) But today, that conviction was sorely tested. We had a lousy tea. I had wanted to tell Jane some things about my work, but there were interminable complaints from the children. I sat there silently stewing. All that can be said for my conviction about the Kingdom is that I didn't burst out in anger at the interference.

•

I am not as successful career-wise as I had expected to be by this time. But how important is that success? Answer: Not much. It's not the be-all and end-all for me. I have some desire for it. I'd like to be recognized, acclaimed. However, contrary to what I thought in my teens and twenties, career success is not the main thing for me. What's more important is peace and contentment in my family. I speak of contentment not just in the sense of a comfortable, tranquil life, although this is desirable, but in the sense of sharing life, passing it on, nurturing these young lives mentally, physically, emotionally and spiritually—in the way that Jane and I do for each other. Thus, family life is the focus of a growing, deepening spiritual life leading me ever more into God. Time and again, it has struck me after a lot of hassle and anxiety about my twisted desires and *bêtises*: the most important thing after all is to be at peace with your family. That is success—the major one, the most important one.

Besides, when appraising my lack of career success, I often see it not in terms of my own values, but in terms of the judgement of others. But surely the people whose opinions matter to me would recognize on a moment's reflection that I have the success that counts.

4

Life and Death

I think a lot about death. Whether this is just a tendency to morbidity or whether it is a truly spiritual and Gospel-oriented reflection, I don't know. What's the point of thinking about death, trying to prepare yourself for it before it happens? You never know what it's going to be like, so why not just forget about it? Well, I think that trying to be as realistic as possible about death has a lot to do with directing you towards a better life.

The best way to think about death is in the context of the marvellous yet terribly fragile gift of life. It's only when we face the extreme implausibility, the prodigious giftedness of our life, that we can accept death with any equanimity. And accepting death means recognizing the poverty of our existence, all the poverties and limitations of our nature and circumstances—accepting them joyfully as part of the amazing preciousness of life.

More and more, I find it hard to feel with any certainty that there is an afterlife—one, at least, that I can grasp. I believe our faith's teaching on eternal life, but confronted with the prospect of rotting flesh, the decay of this body, the concept of eternal life is so devoid of any imaginable detail that it is of little comfort to me. Instead of being depressed, though, I feel a much greater appreciation of this life. Deep down, there is an almost delirious joy at knowing that the great gift is to be alive—for any length of time, no matter how short. If God created me to be here for sixty, seventy or eighty years or whatever, and to experience this amazing life for that time, well, so be it. This state of affairs speaks to me of a loving, prodigally generous God, one who created me in a capricious, whimsical burst of joy. As long as I have lived for some short time in the mind of such a God, then that is enough.

Come to that, could I ever cease to exist in the mind of God? I keep thinking of the line in Psalm 103: "But the love of the Lord for those who fear him lasts forever." Maybe that's the sense in which I'm immortal. If God's love for me exists forever, surely I still exist in whatever way matters.

•

The whole point about accepting mortality and the end of my life is surrender. It is giving up the gift of life that matters, not insisting on it or clinging to it. I think basically this is the most religious (the holiest?) attitude—that of the ultimate surrender, the acceptance of the poverty of our existence, of the fact that we don't own it in the long run.

•

On Tuesday, while coming in to work, I was a bit frustrated about the fact that the workload was beginning to weigh me down. While walking down Spadina Ave., I thought: "Well, the main thing is being alive; if I can accomplish just one tiny personal goal such as mailing the parcel to Mother, I will be grateful." I really felt the truth of that. But it turned out to be a terrible day. There were about ten articles on my desk, many phone calls and long, disconcerting sessions with both T. and B. Very hectic on the whole. Although I did get the parcel mailed, I wasn't very joyful about it. Yet I think the truth remains that it is a gift to be alive and the little extras are delightful.

Next day I was left largely alone. Having a morning cup of tea, I sat there marvelling at the reddish brown of the brew against the white china, the clusters of bubbles on the surface, each of them with a gold ring around it reflecting the gold rim of the cup. Beginning to feel very peaceful and to recognize that I was having a lovely day, I recalled that it was my father's birthday.

●

Sunday night after the pizza/bingo at the church, I was feeling very thwarted and impatient about this job, angry that I wasn't accomplishing any of "my" work. It was a reaction to the steady grind of the previous two weeks. But I came upon Metz's *Poverty of Spirit* and was especially touched by his explanation of the way we encounter God in our frustrations, our limitedness, our unfulfilled dreams and ambitions—that this is what it means to be human. So my prayer became an admission to God of how cross I felt about it all, that I was really resenting this "poverty." Gradually, I got some peace while thinking about what the temptations of Jesus meant, what the beatitudes really mean: accepting our human limitations, living the life God sends us, instead of trying to control everything so that we can fill ourselves with riches.

●

I want to emphasize this point: the way to live is to "Let go and let God", as they say in Alcoholics Anonymous. To let go of my ego, my plans. To rejoice in what comes along. Even though I often seem to know myself less and less, and to have a very poor sense of what's good for me, it doesn't really matter. God, through the incidents of life, is shaping me as God sees fit. The things God sends are really so much better than I could imagine. This outlook fits with what I understand as "poverty of spirit" as described by Metz and with the *via negativa* as delineated by Matthew Fox.

What amazes me is that it seems a true and deep experience of the old spirituality about letting go of the self, relinquishing of self-will and so on. There is this difference, though. In the past, I would have tried to live out such self-denial as a very wilful and determined attempt to become holier and more perfect. Now, on the contrary, I see it as a joyful, carefree, relaxed surrender of my preciously guarded goals and identity. What matters is to let God do the work that's to be done, how and when God likes. This surrender includes, of course, the realization that God is apparently not intending to craft any finely polished jewel of religious perfection out of me. And that this is just fine with me. Accepting that is the bottom line of poverty of spirit.

•

I suspect that, when death comes, you never have a feeling of satisfaction, of the fullness of life. Basically, you're terribly aware of your emptiness, your poverty. The only way to go is to resign yourself to the poverty of your existence, to hand it back to God. Therein lies the beauty, the richness of life. Some would find my saying this ironic in the light of L.'s legacy to me. Even so, I'm struck by the fact that even with a full, busy and enjoyable life such as she had, there are many things she wanted to do but couldn't. She didn't make much use of her money in the end.

•

The preacher was talking about a man he'd been asked to visit twenty-five years ago. The man had been successful but was dying of cancer at the age of forty-one. He had no hope. The man felt as though black walls were closing in on him, said the preacher. Since the Mass was so crowded, we were sitting on the bench along the side wall of the church. This position gave me a different view of everybody. I was observing a young guy sitting opposite us—a hearty bachelor-type who didn't look particularly devout or spiritual. I got to thinking about him on his deathbed and how everything would zero in on his thoughts and his feelings. Whoever was with him would try to pay the utmost attention to him and deal with whatever was important to him. Then I thought of M.'s statement about how, when his inoperable brain tumour was diagnosed, he found his attention focused on the things that really matter.

So I was thinking about the Christmas holidays and how it gets so frantic trying to decide what to do next. There are many conflicting desires and demands. I was reminded that what is really important and valuable is to spend time with the children and Jane, to be present to family and friends. If death were imminent, these would be the things that would matter. It would not matter whether or not I had finished reading the newspaper or had bought a shirt.

•

It's not that buying a shirt or reading the paper have no value. These activities are integral and (sometimes) enjoyable parts of my life. They have their place in daily living. I don't want to be the kind of "spiritual" person who disparages this human business. The point is that, during the holidays, it seemed more worthwhile to take the rare opportunity to be with family at some length. It was not so important to get that day's paper read. As for the shirt, I can get by with what I have. It's not so important to get another one right now.

•

Yesterday, an old man shuffled past the office window, all bundled up against the cold. He was well-dressed, but didn't look very healthy or vigorous. I thought: what a pity at his age to have to battle with infirmity when one should be enjoying retirement. Then it occurred to me that life is a struggle, it always will be, and I think *it's actually meant to be*. That's what it is to be human. Yet we, or at least I, always want to be a god: to have complete serenity, peace, security, comfort, pleasure at all times. But this is to try to shuck off being human and not let God be God. We have to be dependent on God. This is not to say that I'm espousing any masochistic, penitential, self-sacrificing attitude. Rather, it's a very profound, radical acceptance of our inescapable weakness, our infirmity, our need to rely on God for our happiness. This is the essence and the joy of being human.

What may have produced this thought was praying on John 14: "a peace the world does not give." It struck me in a new way what this means. The world cannot know you, the world "hates" you, not because you're a sanctimonious martyr, but rather because you accept weakness, dependency on God. These are not the values of consumerism, career-ism, advertising and so on. This interpretation enables me to accept that the "world" can "hate" us but that I don't hate the people of the world. I can love them very well, while understanding why they don't love what I see as the meaning of life.

•

One day, while sitting on our bed reading, I saw a pigeon winging its way across the rooftops. It seemed so businesslike and purposeful. Where was it going and why? To get a drink? To find a better source of food? To add a twig to its nest? What struck me was that the movements of a bird, seemingly aimless or whimsical to us, actually have a very definite purpose both from the point of view of the bird and in the overall scheme of things, that is, in God's view. So it struck me that all our to-ing and fro-ing, the busy-ness that sometimes seems pointless, has meaning and purpose in God's plan. In other words, we don't need to denigrate the little acts that make up so much of our lives: picking up our clothes at the dry cleaner's, shovelling the snow, emptying the wastebaskets. It's all part of the business of being alive and expressing the life of God in us as we're meant to.

•

Although there are several attitudes in the J. H. G. journal that I don't share, I do respond heartily to a couple of points. First, he says that you accept and rejoice in whatever weather comes. You don't wish for anything different. I've been learning this lately. The erratic quality of the weather used to bother me greatly (because of my poor adaptability to change). But, a few months ago, I was very struck by F.'s saying that what interests him about the weather is the fact that it's always changing. Lately, I've been enjoying this too. From the many personal memoirs I've been reading lately, it's obvious that the weather always has been, and always will be, extremely variable. My longing for the idyll, my false memories of the past and my literary impressions of the set piece used to make me want permanence. It now seems that each new shift in the weather is another expression of God's life in the world in a way that is especially interesting, because it's one of the few phenomena of nature that people don't yet have much control over.

•

The other point from the J. H. G. journal that appeals to me: he says you just let it happen. According to him, Merton said that you don't go rushing around to find what's already there. I love that. It feels exactly right.

•

After working at patching the bathroom wallpaper—none too successfully—it occurred to me that doing home repairs is like writing stories or any other art, indeed, like the art of life itself: you have to learn to live with your mistakes, your limitations, your failures. You're never going to enjoy what success you have if you flagellate yourself for the slip-ups. In other words, you can't insist on perfection in yourself and your works.

•

Further on this business of gratitude for existence, for the gift of life: this awareness induces a kind of pleasure, or, let's say, appreciation, at the thought of getting up and going to work in the morning. This is so even when I'm not very energetic, possibly even depressed or anxious. It is satisfying just to remember that I'm alive and that these daily rituals express the gift of another day of life. Also, of course, there is the gratitude that I have a job and that I'm physically and mentally able to do it.

The point here is not that I'm comparing my lot to that of people who are unemployed or incapacitated. The point is, rather, gratefulness for the realities, the details of my life, whatever they may be. For all I know, the unemployed and disabled may be able to find such details in their own lives to appreciate. (Not that I want to switch places with them!)

•

I was thinking about the old idea of "resignation" to the will of God. That wording suggests a self-mortifying grimness. Isn't it rather a process of opening yourself up, with excitement and joy, to discovering what God has in store, how God's universe will unfold? Not, of course, that you always feel the excitement and joy, but aren't they at least as plausible as dour "resignation"?

•

At the cottage, I sat down to look closely at the butterfly weed (which I had thought was Indian paintbrush), soaking up the flower's brilliant orange and its intricate structure. I had a brief flash of the feeling of being in touch with God that peering into the mystery of things sometimes gives me. A moment like this nourishes my faith deep in the well of "unknowing" (to borrow a term from the mystics). By this I mean it is the mystery of the flower that affects me. My appreciation of nature isn't an automatic piety that leaps from the flower to some fantasy about its Creator. Rather, it's a simple absorption in the living thing itself, with the recognition that, marvellous as it is to learn about, I can never fully understand it. This "ungraspableness" is the expression of God, the presence of God. Life itself is God's presence. But it's in inanimate things too—as the rocks, clouds and water here at Georgian Bay show.

•

On our last morning at the cottage, Jane was awakened about four-thirty by a bumping sound, so she woke me and asked me to check the boat. The sound turned out to be coming from another island. Unable to get back to sleep, I got up around five-thirty and went out. Jane persuaded me to take a thin blue blanket. Light was just beginning to seep into the darkness. You could make things out, but they were greyish and shadowy. When stepping over rocks, you might misjudge the distance or depth. I sat on a low spot on the diving/fishing rock. It was chilly enough that I was glad of the blanket as well as my jacket and sweater. I'd barely sat down when a dark triangle came slicking up out of the flat water in front of me. It was a fish feeding on insects. The whole time that I was in the area, it kept jumping every few minutes and making noisy splashes.

The islands and the mainland to the east were black, hulking, barely green. In the channel were billowing clouds of mist, a few trees jutting through. By now, the sky was a deep reddish orange at the base, fading upwards to gold, then pale blue. The water wasn't so much water as the play and dance of colour in God's mind: pink, turquoise, blue, silver, green—all rippling and merging gently. To the west, hovered a huge clump of cumulous clouds, mostly leaden gray, but luminous white here and there.

A goose flew overhead, but long before seeing it, I could hear the squeaky swish of its wings coming up from behind. Feeling very connected to the physical world, I thought of P. and D. and their bodies in the repose of death, settling into the earth. I could see how you had to surrender your body, to let it sink back into the earth, to let it become part of the earth again. Lying on the rock, I almost felt that I was rising up out of my body, giving it to the earth, and thus becoming one with the whole world.

•

I can't pretend ever to have experienced the kind of darkness or the abandonment Thomas Merton describes in *Contemplative Prayer*. But I do have a disposition to accept my nothingness, to confront the emptiness of existence. It can suddenly come over me while sitting down to a plain supper on a dull day. It's a Lenten feeling: the stark emptiness of the desert. Such boredom is a natural part of living. What's important is to accept it in a religious spirit—not to rail against life for failing to provide you with constant thrills. What I'm talking about is trying to cultivate the spirit of poverty. In prayer, I don't demand satisfaction or try to control what happens. At the cottage, when I felt so poorly, I just let it be.

•

After reading the article by the widow of the activist who died of brain cancer, I found that one point made quite an impression on me. The widow talked about how, in the months preceding his death, the two of them prayed Psalm 131 and adopted the Psalm's attitude—abandoning thoughts of lofty projects and ambitions, just sitting quietly, content in the Lord, putting anxiety aside. Much as I love that Psalm, it never struck me before how perfectly appropriate it would be in the face of death. Much more so, I think, than Psalms like the twenty-third, in which you work yourself up to a point of courage, or try to console yourself with beautiful images. Not that there's anything wrong with any of the Psalms, but Psalm 131 seems perfect in the face of imminent death—just waiting, being open. The *profound* faith it expresses: no insights, no expectations whatsoever, rather simple trust like that expressed by Thérèse Martin.

At some point recently, when I was fussed up about something, I found myself thinking of what the widow said about that Psalm. It helped to quiet my mind, to still the turbulent efforts to sort things out, the relentless attempt to arrive at insights or conclusions.

•

The news has arrived of the deaths of D. L. and W. B., both people I knew only slightly. For some reason, I feel stunned by these deaths. Perhaps in part because both were sudden deaths and the people were quite young (sixty or less). The fact is, although I often talk about death with resignation and acceptance, I cannot *truly* imagine my own death. I can fantasize about it, but appreciating the reality and inevitability of it is quite another matter. The fact that this life of mine would just suddenly stop and that this flesh would corrupt and decay and become nothing—no, that is unthinkable!

And yet, even while writing this, I feel a kind of peace and acceptance. It is the very unthinkability of death—the unimaginable bizarreness of it—that gives me a kind of release. The concept of death is simply beyond me. Death is not something any of us would ever have planned if we were organizing the universe. Our own ephemerality is not an outcome we could ever have expected or wanted. So life is much more mysterious, more precious than we could ever have imagined. In the face of such a great, awesome, impenetrable mystery, all we can do is lovingly surrender ourselves to the care of the Father with gratefulness for this precious gift, and with confidence that he knows how to handle it. (Psalm 103: The Lord's love for those who fear him lasts from eternity and forever.)

•

The passion narratives in Matthew: I used to hate those lugubrious readings. Now, however, I'm struck by the pathetic, impoverished, abused humanity of Jesus. For instance, his refusal to drink the vinegar: it struck me that he's not inviting suffering, he's not going to play the clown for them. He's hanging on to whatever integrity he can.* Then: "Why have you abandoned me?" I identify so strongly with the depression, the anguish. Life looks so black—hanging there naked, hardly able to breathe, insulted. How could you feel other than abandoned? No love at all in the world. The tiny spark that sustains you, that makes you feel wanted and needed, has almost been snuffed out.

•

I feel more than ever resigned to the fact that, not speaking at all pessimistically, life is a series of problems to encounter and to live through. I don't mean that life is a question of *solving* problems, of moving onto a plateau at which all problems have been resolved. There will always be more. Many of them you never really solve; you just learn to cope with them. I no longer feel that one is striving constantly to reach a problem-free existence, whether as a result of moral

---

*   Or am I mistaken in my interpretation of the vinegar? It seems to me that some commentators have said it was offered as an anaesthetic. If so, his refusing it would be the opposite of my interpretation—he declined a means of escape from suffering.

worth, effort, good luck or whatever. This is not to say that life does not have lots of pleasures. It does. Looked at in one way, you could say those pleasures are the main point of life. But you will be free to enjoy them more if you accept the concomitant problems that are constant in life, accept them with equanimity, and do not spoil your enjoyment by futile longing for pure pleasure and deliverance from all problems.

•

One of the things that is becoming most apparent about our life here in France is that it's an exercise in accepting the poverty of our existence. "Poverty?" you say, "You have a pile of money to see you through the year. You don't have to earn a cent!" True, but the elimination of financial worries points up the real poverty of life: the limitations of time and space. There are so many things I want to do this year, each day, and I can hardly get any of them done: travel, sight-seeing, reading, writing, painting, drawing, walking, being with the family, praying, playing music and listening to it, studying French and practising it . . . .

You have to throw up your hands and simply say: OK, whatever is given to me to do each day, no matter how little, I shall enjoy it and be glad of the opportunity. That is what I mean about the poverty of our existence, the limitations of being human, the impossibility of ever satisfying all our desires. This year of retreat is showing us how little any human life amounts to. Perhaps that awareness is integral to any genuine retreat. (You can bet that when Jesus was in the desert he didn't accomplish a whole lot; his day wasn't crammed with gratifying religious exercises!) Accepting this (sometimes excruciating) limitation and being grateful for life all the same is living in the spirit of poverty.

•

Further to this business of poverty of spirit, it needs to be said that, underlying the acceptance of not being able to do everything you want, is the acceptance of the ultimate poverty—death. You're going to die without having accomplished everything you'd like, without having amassed as much wealth as you wanted, without having been all the places and done all the things you dreamed of—even without having loved as much and as fully as you wish you had. But you can accept this and say: OK, Lord, if you say that's enough, it's enough. That acceptance is what underlies the everyday spirit of poverty. We don't own anything. It's all given by God. Without this fundamental outlook, exhortations to be contented with one day at a time would be relatively trite and banal. Recognition of the ultimate poverty—mortality—gives profound meaning to the acceptance of the little poverties of each day.

•

The whole trip took four hours.[*] I was walking very slowly because of incipient flu. It felt as though each of my legs weighed a ton. With every step, I seemed to sink further into the earth. Forcing myself to breathe deeply, in spite of my partially stuffed nose, I began to be very conscious of my lungs working—all that spongy, damp pink tissue pumping in and out. I became aware of myself as a physical creature with the strengths and limitations that implies. The main limitation—mortality. I could imagine breathing my last breath—my lungs swelling and contracting for the last time. Surprisingly, the thought came with considerable equanimity. It felt possible that I could be content to give up my last breath—when the time comes—to return to matter. A sense of what it would be like simply to resign myself, to let myself go, flowed over me.

You go back to God with empty hands. You have nothing. It's not a question of being content to die because you've accomplished so much or you've left

---

[*]   Because of a postal strike in our region of France, I had to walk to another village, five miles away, to mail our Christmas letters.

behind such an impressive testament (literary or whatever), or you've left such indelible foot marks. No, not
at all. Your life could be cut off in mid-sentence when
you haven't accomplished any of the things you
wanted. When God says that is enough, that is enough.
You have had the gift of life itself to enjoy, the gift of
being you—a uniquely loved person—and when the
time comes you can willingly let go.

None of this sermonizing guarantees that I'll go
through the process of dying with perfect tranquillity.
If there's pain, I'll be as miserable and cowardly as anybody. And there may be last-minute fears too. But that
doesn't negate the underlying attitude of resignation.

•

A weird day yesterday. Mild nausea kept me from
doing anything much—which was very frustrating
because there are lots of letters to write, not to mention
other projects. The reading for the morning was Matthew 15: "This people worships me with words, but
their heart is really far from me." What does it mean to
worship with the heart? It seems to mean that I must
listen to my heart, not rush ahead feverishly with my
obsessive projects, but wait and rest and let things be.

After tea, I went for a walk. A soft, pinkish sunset.
Stopped by the ruined towers on a little mound surrounded by greenery. Smells of pine, thyme, lavender—thrilling. Sat and looked at the sky, my back
against one of the towers. Prayed. The thought that
came to me was: it doesn't matter about my plans and
projects; basically I'm a little insect crawling along in
God's world—God is running the show and it doesn't
matter about my marvellous plans. I don't need to
bother my head about them any more than the beetle
does; I just need to plod along through the day, doing
whatever I can from one minute to the next. And that
gave me a lot of peace.

While I was praying this morning, an extension of
that thought came: I don't want any great, exciting

insights in prayer; I can't handle them. All I ask is ordinariness, peace, the strength, the willpower, the love to go on living. It was very satisfying to realize that I didn't seek any exciting breakthrough, any great "consolation" in prayer. Of course, you have to admit that to realize you don't need any great insight is itself an insight and a consolation.

•

On the hike to the monastery ruins, I found myself fantasizing about what life there would have been like in the seventeenth century, when the place was in its heyday. I was longing to have lived then, when life was "simpler" and you could be more pure, more dedicated, when there weren't all the distractions of modern life. Then it struck me: how absurd to wish to live in one time rather than another (quite apart from the question of whether conditions in one era would really be more or less agreeable to you than in another era). The important thing is to have lived, to have seen, felt, tasted, made love . . . to be able to know that you are part of all this history, to enjoy life on this earth for your brief moment. You can have fun thinking about the other eras, but to wish to have lived in them is crazy.

•

Last night after supper, I was working on vocabulary from one of the Simenon books. There was a feeling of pressure, as though I must finish this book and many more before leaving France. But suddenly a thought came to me: if Patrick Donohue dies tonight without finishing his vocabulary list, has he not led a worthwhile and rewarding life? Is there any reason why I have to finish vocabulary lists for ten or twenty books as opposed to five or six before we leave France? In other words, if I am doing what I can for now, and it is rewarding and fulfilling, I'm wasting time and mental energy fussing about what I'm not getting done. God is with me here and now. My life is valuable minute by minute, in this very minute. Completing this or that project isn't going to make it more valuable.

I felt very deeply the presence of God within me in a quiet, sustaining way. The pressure of a lot of decisions lifted. It's not important to scheme and plot in order to cram as much as possible into this year. The important thing is to LIVE THE MOMENT and see what God has in it for me. This is the answer to a lot of muddle about the overwhelming number of options for spending my time.

•

The key is to *remain free*. Which is not to say that you just drift and do virtually nothing. On the contrary, you listen closely for the Spirit's promptings as to what you should do in any particular moment. But you must be content with that moment and not be distracted by all the other things you wish you could get done. You will find out in the moment what is important to do. Realizing this, I am much more aware of the presence of God with me than I have been in the last month or so.

•

This morning I was anxious about a number of little errands, about bad dreams and so on. But after meditating a while, I remembered last night's feeling of contentment, and the peace came back to me even more deeply. The Gospel passage for meditation was Matthew 19, about the little children: "The kingdom of heaven belongs to such as these." What joy that phrase brought to me, ringing over and over in my heart. It seemed to express something deep and essential and true, something that is in me, something I must try to hang onto and nurture.

Fundamentally, it is the recognition of life as a gift, the trust and belief that interesting things will turn up, the spirit of remaining open to them. I remember when Madeleine was around three years old, how she was happy to get up every day, with no plan whatsoever, trusting that interesting and entertaining things would come up, that our loving presence would sustain her. That is the spirit of child-likeness that the Gospel speaks of, I think.

Then I was thinking of the great saint of spiritual childhood—Thérèse Martin. She trusted that God was there and that it didn't matter whether she was feeling any special effects of his attention, any shafts of "divine" consolation. Life itself, trying to get along with people, was sufficient. This trust is surely the significance of the dark period at the end of her life when she couldn't "feel" God anymore and even had trouble believing in eternal life. This is a terribly important point in the interpretation of her life. Without this dark time, you wonder whether she could really be considered a saint. Perhaps just a pious little thing with a religious gift. But in this dark period, she anticipates the condition of the twentieth century person who meets life head-on and doesn't ask for any other explanation, who knows that life itself is as close as we can hope to get to seeing and understanding God for now. There is no escape to a world of pleasant religious sentiment. I don't see her, then, as struggling against the dark like a warrior slaying dragons. Rather, as humbly accepting the mundane, the commonplace-ness of our existence, knowing that this is where God puts us and this is where we find the meaning of life. Even though it is difficult getting along with people, she trusts that the process is worthwhile because this is where we meet God, not because we may ultimately be rewarded by some big daddy on high for putting up with these miserable bastards down here.

I don't suppose, though, that it would have occurred to her to explain herself in such terms. If she were to articulate her attitude, she might sound as if she were referring to some very spiritual and "other-worldly" god of the nineteenth century.

•

Meditation this morning on the rich young man, Matthew 19—so many things, a rich passage, worth several days. But the thing that impressed me most today was the comparison between riches and poverty. Why are riches bad? What is good about being poor? Well, from my little experience of riches, I have some idea of the problems involved—you get snarled up in decisions, worries about what to do with the money, in priding yourself on what you have, yet wishing you had more, envying those who do . . . .

Then I got thinking about the aspects of poverty for us this year.* The physical deprivations: the lack of a bath tub, not always getting the food we want, not having sufficient heat in the house much of the time. I don't make much of those deprivations; to do so would be reminiscent of the Spartan idea of self-denial, the old idea of depriving oneself during Lent. But they may be useful in so far as they make you more grateful for what you do have. When you're not surrounded by heat all the time, you appreciate being able to snuggle up to the heater. You enjoy it more.

The more important poverties, however, are the lack of friends, the lack of admirers, the inability (because of linguistic limitations) to be smart, charming and witty, the lack of a lot of exciting outlets and stimulating diversions, the lack of transportation and the consequent restrictions on movement. I'm forced to try to make friends with people whom I wouldn't otherwise seek out. Hence I reach out to someone who may be lonely. (After all, the most popular people in town don't need our friendship.) Jane and I are forced to pay more attention to each other and to the kids. We spend more time with them. Confronted by our boredom, we realize our limitations; we support each other in our slumps. All of this opens us up to the truly human values, helping us to grow, building up the Kingdom of

---

*   In France.

God through the nurturing of each person and helping that person to blossom.

Then, of course, there are the even more profound poverties: the fact that I get so little done each day as opposed to my great plans, the fact that time slips through my fingers. Ultimately the most basic poverty: that each breath I take is not my own, that I owe my life to God, that my life is sustained by God at each moment, that suddenly it will be over, that it will not matter what projects I have completed or not completed. What will matter is how I have lived in relation to others, whether or not I have helped them to discover God within themselves—not by lecturing or writing great things, but simply by being present to them in a true, Christian way.

•

In Bellet, I was really struck by a reference to breathing as life, as the gift of the Spirit. With every breath I take, I am expressing the life of the Spirit. I am expressing the life of God even without thinking of it. This is constant prayer. I think of this when I see the kids in bed at night and I lean over them and hear their breathing. What a precious gift this breath is. I feel their heads—the marvellous weight of them—and I think of all the intricate organs packed in there and their incalculably complex operations. All this has developed from two minuscule morsels of tissue. What a marvellous gift life is. They bring us so much pleasure, these children. No matter how precious, though, their life is tenuous; we don't hold them very tight. (All this within ten minutes of being very angry with them!)

•

Saturday, I was sitting in the backyard watching Michael work on the eaves troughs. It was a bit exasperating trying to keep an eye on him and prevent him from doing dangerous things. I was getting rather discouraged because there were so many problems—the damage to the chimney by the raccoons, the leak in the corner of the trough, the fact that the troughs are not draining properly. I noticed a bit of mortar was missing between two bricks in the back wall of the house. Then I noticed that the line of bricks seemed to be sagging here and there. Then I recalled the plaster which is cracking in many places in the house. Maybe the whole house is falling down? What if the place is ruined? What if it wipes out all our savings trying to fix it? Could I face such disaster?

I picked up a dandelion and held it in the full sunlight. I noticed the fuzzy stamens, brushed them against my cheek, caught the buttery smell of the flower. What about it? Could I be content to have lived, to have seen such beauty, to have enjoyed it, even though some major catastrophe occurred, such as the falling down of my house? Well, it wouldn't be easy. It would be nearly crushing. But ultimately, I could at least try to accept the gift of life the way Job did. It seemed that I could realize that the important thing was to have lived, to have been me, even if something that seemed terribly important to me were wrenched from me.

Maybe I'm kidding myself. Maybe I'd go completely nuts. But I can at least, at this point, claim honestly that I recognize Job's attitude as the best one. The "correct" one? No—the healthiest, the most appreciative of life, the most in touch with reality, the most conducive to one's true happiness. And it's not a matter of intellectual recognition of a theory. It's something in my bones, in my spirit—for now, at least.

•

After debating for weeks about contacting D., I pushed doubts aside and called. She suggested lunch. Jane joined us. D. looked lovely, her eyes sparkling. When we were settled in the restaurant, after checking out how long since we'd seen her (six years), she asked if we'd heard any news about her. We hadn't. So she told us, with some hesitancy but very simply, that P. (her husband) had died of cancer five years ago, just six months after a lump was discovered. He wasn't even forty years old. We expressed our shock but carried on with lunch in a merry tone and parted from her with just a final expression of regret about her difficulties.

Back at home, as the afternoon wore on, the fact of his death sank in. I began to appreciate the horror of what she must have been through. Her apparent happiness now tends to make you underestimate the devastation. It seems easy to say your husband died five years ago, but at the time her life must have been falling apart.

A few things dawned on me in the aftermath of the news. First of all—that life is not about success, about going from one triumph to another. As his death and her loss show, life is about terrible defeat and pain, about meeting disaster head-on. This message was reinforced at our group meeting that night. It was staggering to see the difficulty the members are suffering through, mostly because of their kids.

If life is not about success and gratification in your triumphs, there must be another meaning. Love? Well, ultimately that's the answer, but at times it's too much to ask of anybody. Openness, acceptance, perhaps? You have to come to the point where you can say that, in spite of the tragedy of P.'s early death, his life was good, that it was beautiful for him to have lived, that however much of life is allotted to us is enough. So we have to simply let it happen (life and death), however it will.

Another thing—D.'s loss made me feel a lot closer to her. Somehow, a death like that makes the survivors cling to each other. Each of us shares a little in the loss, the shock, the pain. His death reminds us that we are all mortal. I think this makes us appreciate one another more.

•

On the way to the coffee shop this morning, my heart was jumping irregularly. Would a cup of coffee induce a heart attack? Maybe I would die today. This would be the last day of my life. That felt appalling. In theory, I accept that I can die any time without any warning. I know (supposedly) that my life could be cut off abruptly at any point. But today? A ghastly thought. I haven't accomplished anything. I'm right in the middle of everything. I'm all potential. The world hasn't yet accepted me and recognized me for what I am. Yet . . . what is life about, really? Isn't it about simply living, making the most of the day? What difference would it make if I didn't finish this or that project? Not much. I have to live with that awareness, to appreciate that my relationships with my family and with God are the essence of my life.

•

This morning, I was feeling depressed and disgruntled, as is becoming usual lately. It didn't seem that there was any pleasure to be had from living. During a brief prayer period after making the porridge, this thought came to me: I will have an opportunity today to do something that will give some point for living; there will be a chance to be patient, encouraging with someone; to help someone with something; I will have a chance to "pass on life" to someone. That thought helped relieve the dreariness. Mind you, I turned right around and acted churlishly within five minutes, but on the whole, the day turned out well. Not that I felt tremendously happy, but I felt more resigned, at peace with the situation.

•

One morning recently when praying, I had a very sharp and clear realization of the might-not-have-been quality of my existence. I can't remember now what brought it on. But I was suddenly and deeply struck by the wonder, the miracle, of my existence here and now.

In that moment, I felt a very still, deep presence of God's life sustaining me from within. It was as if I drank slowly and deeply for a few moments from the cool stream of God's life-giving love. It was not the kind of rapturous experience of God's love sometimes felt in the past. It was more like a state of being, not feeling, in awe before the *is* of myself and of God. Coming out of it, I felt that, from now on, I would surely see all of life as a gift, and that nothing could happen to discourage me or take away my joy in the awareness of God's loving life within.

However, the day turned out to be more difficult than usual. I was very tired and irritable and my fine awareness of the morning lasted only as a conviction rather than any satisfying or rewarding experience.

•

The other night T. was absent from the group meeting because of the flu. R. (his wife) described how he was white as a sheet, sweating. He'd had a lot of diarrhoea and other problems. Next day, I was thinking: what if T. died? Not that I really thought he was likely to; it was just that her description of his condition brought home very vividly our mortality. So when praying, meditating throughout the day, I very often thought about what it would mean if a guy like T. suddenly died on us. What would our reactions be? After the shock, we would talk about what a fine guy he was, how he'd done so much good, achieved such virtue, raised a fine family and all that. We'd find meaning in the "fullness" of it all.

But that's not the point, somehow. I kept seeing him pale and drawn, haggard, mortal, dying. It did not look like a very edifying, meaningful death. And so I was thinking: the meaning is simply that he lived, he died. He was cut off when he wanted to achieve much more, grow more, become more loving, holier, happier, healthier. He didn't. But that is the poverty of our existence. We cannot turn at the end of our life and say: "See how much I have achieved? Now my death will be the fitting culmination!" Anybody who says that doesn't understand; they're kidding themselves or missing the point. No matter when you die, at the final moment you don't have anything; you go empty-handed, no matter how much you thought you had achieved. For the most productive, successful person in the world, death is a cutting off, a letting go of all that.

As for T., we can point to especially good moments in his life, be thankful for them, for the relationships he had with us, for the life of the Spirit that he passed on. In this sense we celebrate his life. But we can't pretend that dying is not a process of being stripped, naked and poor. Even in terms of virtues acquired, you have to let go. Who needs them after death? Our lives are like water that trickles through our fingers—all that matters is the refreshment it gives to us and to others, the cooling and the pleasure—when the water goes, our hands are dry, empty; we contain nothing, we are the breath of wind that is gone.

The point of all this is that it is fatuous to attempt to make sense of death by trying to add up a dead person's achievements and attributes in order to show that the deceased's life was worthwhile. That makes a mockery of life. I was going to say that this is what the obituary columns are full of. But, to be fair, it's only the obits of the rich and famous that reflect such thinking. Obits of ordinary folk usually focus on loving relationships.

When praying at dusk, looking out at the bleak winter sky and the stark trees, feeling the emptiness of the hour, the dullness, the apathy, I was very much aware of this possibility of a middle-aged friend's dying. The mood was a confrontation with the fact that we are poor creatures; when all's said and done, we don't have much to show. It is good to confront this emptiness, this feeling of poverty, to acknowledge the fragility of our existence.

●

We are swept up in the great river of life/love. That is the important thing—we are part of it, we enjoy it, we experience it. That is what we celebrate at the end of somebody's life—the fact that he or she floated along with us for a while in this great river and shared the joy of it with us. That's far more important to us than particular accomplishments.

I'm not saying that the individual is of no importance. The particular traits of a person—the good ones as well as the bad, the pleasant as well as the not-so-pleasant—form a part of the overall picture and we appreciate them as such. It is the uniqueness of each person which makes that person so precious. But that does not mean that at death we add up the assets of that individual as if they could somehow justify that person's life. That's ridiculous, though perhaps a natural tendency.

One of the reasons why it's patently absurd is that this reckoning would "prove" that the life of some big operator who accomplished a lot was more valuable than the life of some seemingly inconsequential person. And this would obviously be an intolerable conclusion, from my point of view, and, I think, from the point of view of the Gospel of Jesus. I would go so far as to say that the life of a person who shows great moral worth is not really any more valuable in God's eyes than the life of someone who leads a fairly humdrum life, a life as closely in tune with true human values as is possible for that person within his or her given limits, but not a life notable for any spiritual or moral accomplishment. For that matter, is anybody's life any more or less valuable in God's eyes than anyone else's life? I think not.

The only point in talking about the notably good qualities of someone's life, I guess, is that they help to point out to us what is good and desirable about our life as humans. If this is what is meant by singing the praises of the dead—that they serve as reminders to us of the way to live—then there's nothing wrong with doing so.

But listing a dead person's merits doesn't amount to some sort of justification of that person's existence. Such an attempt to counteract apparent annihilation by death would be futile. The only consolation in the face of the stripping, the destruction of death, is to accept it joyfully in the same spirit of poverty in which the gift of life is accepted.

•

Last night while I was tucking Michael in, he was asking me about the night twelve years ago.* He was lying there beaming, he loved hearing about it. He wanted to know how far apart the labour pains were. I said the doctor decided to do a cesarean delivery because it was taking too long. Michael asked, "Because I was too big?"

I remembered hearing about someone who lost her first baby, a boy, because the delivery took too long. And I realized once again how glad I am that we didn't lose this baby. Thinking of all that has happened in the twelve years since his birth, I felt very deeply in my heart how right and good his life with us has been.

Imagine this unborn baby (Michael, myself, or any of us), a squirming thing inside his mother's womb, not knowing what was happening to him, not knowing whether his life was in danger or not. How precarious life is. The basic response is simply to be grateful for it. Not to question or complain. Admittedly, you have to learn to handle your swings of mood, your irritations and the inevitable problems. You can't expect to be joyful all the time.

•

My impression after visiting the funeral home is that the family hadn't wanted us to show up. Still, I wanted to do something to acknowledge their father's death. What struck me about the situation is that this

---

*   The eve of his birth.

death of someone close brings on a terrible dread, a recognition of the awful poverty of our existence, of the fact that we don't own our lives and they're going to be snatched from us. It is this common plight that you want to acknowledge by showing up and willingly taking on a little bit of their pain, confronting it, sharing the darkness—rather than skulking around and pretending you don't know about the death in their family or don't want to disturb them by saying anything.

•

Today, I was wondering whether or not I should really say that my life is going to end. After all, that seems to run counter to Christian dogma. But, while finishing up a coffee at the donut shop, it occurred to me: I might as well say my life is going to end because there is damn little I can say about any life after this. Life *as I know it* will end. As for a new life, the imagination fails utterly.

But here's the point: *trust*. That's what it's all about. Many of us claim to have "faith" in the afterlife. But it's not faith; it's more like superstition. It's wanting to cling to some comforting formula, to fantasies that are pretty ludicrous. The more religious approach would be to say, "I haven't a clue what will happen; it's all in God's hands; I trust God." Most people want to appropriate the knowledge of an afterlife to themselves rather than leave it in God's hands.

5

Sin, Guilt, and Forgiveness

In the past, much of the preaching about sin wasn't about real sin at all. It was about rule-breaking and losing face. It was meant to alienate you from yourself, to make you hate yourself, make you feel inferior to the authority who defined the sin in you. After breaking free from a scrupulosity induced by that kind of training, I lived several years with little or no sense of personal sin. Now, I am beginning to see real sin (not anything much like what I previously thought) in my life. I can proclaim, willingly and without any cloying sense of self-loathing, "Yes, Lord, I am a sinner."

Forgiving myself means something quite different from what I used to think. It means not trying to analyze my mistake overly much, to explain it away, to point to some cause, as if to say, "But for that factor, the mistake would never have happened because, prescinding from such terrible aggravation, I could not have done such a thing." Instead of all that, forgiving myself means accepting that it happened, that I did it, and then holding myself in two hands and loving myself all the same. In the past, I could forgive myself, as (it seemed) others could forgive me, only if I could separate myself from such and such a flaw or failure. Now I feel that forgiveness means accepting myself even when I let myself down.

•

In the back of my mind during meditation the other day was a recent event that could have made me feel very sinful. The message that came through was that the problem with the troubling incident was simply my failure to love myself enough, to be in touch with God's love for me. I had put myself through a lot of turmoil only because I didn't love myself enough. So there was a sense of guilt, a recognition of sinfulness, of distance from God—but in a totally non-self-incriminating way, a non-self-chastising or self-flagellating way. That deep peace has stayed with me.

Am I refusing to face up to guilt? I don't think so. The message seems very deep and real: that the main thing to learn from the incident is that I must ask God to help me to learn to love myself more. Even when reading Paul's diatribe on guilt and sinfulness, I can see/feel his words in a totally non-self-loathing way. This new approach to sin and guilt is a process of quelling the voice of the scolding nun in me who tries to tell me that I'm a worthless shit. Instead, I am listening to the supportive lover who wants the best for me.

•

Reflection on Psalm 51 helped me a lot—not in a breast-beating, obsessively guilty way—but as a loving, understanding, *even sympathetic*, look, into my soul. I am especially struck by the theme: "Against you only have I sinned and done what is evil in your sight." How deeply it is true that sin, in the sense of acting contrary to my own good, is a betrayal of God within me. It is a denial of what is good and true about me; it is a mutilation of, a violence against, the goodness and beauty of myself. It is a refusal to accept myself as the beautiful person I am. It is turning my back on myself and saying, "I'm not a nice person; I'm ugly, self-destructive."

So sin is fundamentally a wrong done to God within. No matter what the sin and its various consequences, this is the primary thrust of it: "Against you only . . . what is evil in your eyes . . . ."

•

Regarding my feeling guilty about a lack of generosity in family life: perhaps the problem is seeing that lack as selfish or sinful. Instead of feeling guilty about it, it might be better to say, "OK, God, this is the way you made me and I can be quite comfortable with myself, but now you want me to be something better." Then I can avoid the destructive tendency towards self-chastisement when I find myself not living up to my calling. I can be patient and say, "Oh yes, here's old me asserting myself again. Maybe that old lazy me will go away. Or maybe I'll forget about being that way some day. Maybe not. But in the meantime, let's not fret about it."

•

In my meditation this week, for some reason, I have been dwelling on Psalm 51, especially, "Indeed in guilt was I born and in sin my mother conceived me," or as another translation puts it, "You know I was born guilty, a sinner from the moment of conception." I begin to sense that real sin has to do with being totally wrapped up in yourself to the detriment of others and your relationships with them. And what could be more totally wrapped up in itself than a baby? The irony of it is that the baby is absolutely unaware of its utter dependence on others. So it seems to me that we sin as we approach that state of self-centredness and complete disregard of our connectedness with others. Sin is being blind to this reality.

•

To what extent do my actions interfere with the growth and freedom of other people? As I see it, people have sinned against me when they have interfered with my growth, with my becoming who I am meant to be in God's eyes. So I sin when I impose on others my limited, arrogant view of who they should be and how they should act. This is the great sin, the great temptation, in marriage and in family: to impose, to insist on my rightness, my way of doing things. The imposing can, of course, be overt or subtle, even subconscious.

•

Thinking about being in moral trouble: I have to step back, be patient and allow God time to speak to the real me, in other words, to let my real nature speak of itself. Not that the temptations are unreal or illusory. The inclination to sin is real; the feelings are genuine. But they don't define me. They occur at a somewhat superficial level. There is a deeper level of being that is not troubled.

The trouble and confusion are aspects of who I am, but not the basis. It is as if I were a town. There may be turbulent weather and there may be calm weather. These are characteristics of the town at any given moment. But the essence of the town is something more basic: the rocks, the soil, the waters, the houses, the relationships among the townspeople.

•

It surprises me that it can still be such a struggle to be good.* I always thought that you'd be converted for once and for all and that, from there on, it would be a

_____

* The item on pp. 23-24 notes that the good wells up naturally in me, *but* I don't always let it do so!

joy to be good, you would want only to do good. Hence, when I have inclinations to do otherwise, I'm torn between two interpretations of the situation: 1. This can't be me; this can't be this nice Patrick Donohue who is feeling this way; I must have "fallen back" and become a terrible person; 2. What I want in this moment can't be bad since I, this irreproachable person, want it.

When I speak of good and bad here, I am referring to what is or is not life-giving to oneself and others. It has little to do with breaking or following rules.

•

The other morning, there was a flash of white light in my mind and with it came a picture of myself sitting in the sunlight in front of a little house in the country, with flowers around, birds, children playing in the grass. I was surrounded by my loved ones, full of happiness and contentment. The vision, although fleeting, grasped for barely a split second, revealed something deep within me.

That "something" is why I do not go off and do the many immoral and dangerous things I want to do—because there is planted deeply within me this longing for peace and purity. This is the sum total of my religious quest—simply this sense of being able to dwell at peace in my home and my heart. In other words, this is the strongest pull to the Good. This is the basic yearning for God. This is the essence of the quest that the psalmists expressed many times: "For you my soul pines and thirsts . . . "; "Like the deer that yearns"; and so on.

You can forget that deep still voice within you when you become embroiled in worries and frustrations. It is good to be reminded of it. Keeping in touch with it, despite all the frustrations, the vicissitudes, the spoilings, is what is meant by living a life of purity, dedication, loyalty. This is the light that you see in the eye of a saintly Thomas More or whomever.

I realize that this image of the good life looks complacent, passive, narcissistic, self-satisfied. Other people might picture the good life in terms of waging war to better the world, championing the cause of those who need it. I sometimes do think of living this way, especially when I'm reminded of Jean Vanier's love of that wonderful text from Isaiah (58): "Give food to the hungry, relief to the oppressed . . . and your shadows will be as the noon sun."

But that's a secondary image of the good life for me. The primary one is the white cottage: putting my own house in order. (Perhaps the fact that there is nothing of glamour or drama about the image speaks for its authenticity.) It may not express the fullness of a life of Christian service, but it's a starting point: the most fundamental meaning of the expression "charity begins at home."*

•

Many of the things that often seem to loom largest as "sin" are not very important in themselves. You simply have to pray for the good sense not to let them cause disproportionate harm. If these acts are wrong at all, then the way to look at them is this: I am constantly trying to love and heal myself into a healthy state, but sometimes it doesn't work. Is that any reason for self-hatred, for self-loathing? Should you succumb to a sense of guilt that you have been taught—a sense of yourself as a horrible boy who doesn't deserve to see the light of day, who should be put in the corner? No, not at all. In fact, those feelings are a capitulation to discouragement, an excuse for feeling that you can never and will never "be good." Such "guilt" is totally self-defeating and self-destructive. What is called for is not a rapping on the knuckles, but more self-loving. (I

---

* Perhaps people who are more naturally active than I in the pursuit of justice for others don't have to spend as much time as I do to keep their private houses in order?

cannot claim that I always accept my sins this way. There is in me a great residue of the old self-loathing, the naughty-boy complex ready to well up at any time.)

This is not to say that there is no place in my life for true guilt—that is, the recognition that I have truly done wrong, and regret for it. But I think this should be reserved for the kind of thing that seriously interferes with the life of God in people—for example, the times you selfishly thwart people and block God's love from flowing through you to them. However, I don't think this recognition amounts to the kind of guilt that runs and hides from God, that kicks oneself in the backside for being so horrible. Rather, it is the simple awareness of the reality of sin in me: being tied up in myself, my fears, my aggressions, my hostilities. I gladly admit that this is what it means to call myself a sinner. I recognize that this is what Jesus came to liberate me from, and I wholeheartedly ask him to do so.

•

Praying the Jesus prayer,* I find that I can accept fully and gladly the label "sinner." It means that I have this tendency to close in on myself, not to go out of myself and meet people in the exchange that is loving and life-giving. And I have to ask constantly for his help, the infusion of his Spirit to enable me to begin to live in the way that gives life to others.

•

While I was meditating the other day on Jesus' prediction of Peter's denial (Matthew 26), this sentence struck me as very poignant, "You will say that you *do not know me*." Devastating. Not to be known. The feeling of being a stranger. It reminds me of that horrible objectified feeling I get sometimes—a feeling that I'm just a thing, of no interest to anyone. Nothing could be

---

* "Lord Jesus Christ, Son of the Living God, have mercy on me, a sinner."

worse. Consignment to that status by someone you love would be worse than hatred or betrayal.

I used to think that this passage was full of dire foreboding and terrible judgment—showing Peter up for a phoney, a creep, a louse. There seemed to be a kind of bitterness on Jesus' part—"I'm smarter than you; I know you're going to fail the big test, even though you're too stupid and vain to realize now how despicable you really are." But now I don't see it at all that way. Rather, Jesus is saying calmly and lovingly: "I want you to know that I accept and love you no matter what. It is important that you know this beforehand—that even with full knowledge of your character, I have accepted you. Because, in a way, I know you can't help it, this is just what people do. You are weak like all of us. And when it happens, know that it doesn't make any difference to my feelings for you. I don't think any the less of you or love you any less. The fact is, I never have been looking for the strong, infallible hero that you like to think you are."

It is so important to interpret this statement from Jesus as clearing the air before the fact. Otherwise, you have to ask: Why would he say it? Why make his friend feel bad by accusing him of some terrible, unthinkable failing? No, it's not to make him feel bad—although at the moment it would undoubtedly cause him some consternation. It is so that, in the long run, he will know that he has been loved all along, that, as far as Jesus is concerned, the failure of loyalty does not in any way break the relationship—*if Peter doesn't feel that he has broken it*—that is, if he still *wants* to have the relationship, unlike Judas who gave up.

The worst thing about most sin is that it can make you feel sin-*full* if you let it. It can make you feel cut off from God. And how could it do anything so absurd? Largely, I think, because of bad education about sin, the kind of upbringing that drives home the message, "You're a bad, naughty boy." But perhaps such training only reinforces what may be an innate tendency. In the story of Adam's and Eve's fall, the main thing that comes through to me is not so much their transgression, but the way their guilt made them run from God, full of fear, rather than turning to him and seeking to restore the relationship.

•

I decided to meditate this morning on the Prodigal Son, which was the reading at Sunday's Mass. My first reaction, after reading the story over, is one of praise and thanks to God for having given us Jesus, for having put a man among us who could tell such a beautiful, heart-warming, sun-drenched story. It strikes absolutely to the core of what is essential in human life.

An amazing number of details surprised me, as though I were encountering them for the first time: 1. It was a question of the father's giving property and, a few days later, the son selling the property. I'd always assumed it was money the father gave. What kind of property? Land? Did he subdivide the land? Surely it wasn't just goods and chattels—that wouldn't bring in much. But the idea of subdividing the land and selling off part of it is rather more serious. 2. "Wasted his money in reckless living": that is how Jesus described what ensued. It strikes me how mild, how benevolent this assessment of the situation is, compared to the older brother's vituperative, judgemental embroidering of the facts. Jesus is noting sadly what happened without making a big deal of it. 3. It was a severe famine, so he was left without a thing. How does that follow? He did get a job. Then why couldn't he use his wages to buy food? Admittedly there wasn't much, but there was at least enough to feed pigs. Or didn't his employer pay him anything? Why wouldn't it have occurred to him just to take some of the pigs' food? Was he so conscientious? Did the boss watch the feed so closely that he couldn't sneak a bit? Why does he just wait for somebody to give him some? It makes him seem like quite a scrupulous fellow after all. But none of these details is terribly important to the essence of the story. They're interesting by way of pointing up how much one fails to notice when one assumes that one knows all the Bible stories.

And so to the more important points of the story. It seems to me that one of the key sections is: "He came to his senses." He's not doubled over with paroxysms of guilt; he's not exaggerating his sinfulness. He just wakes up and sees the light. And what he sees, first of all, is the difference between his circumstances and those of his father's employees. He simply sees that they've got a better deal than he has. I suspect that there is a dawning of humility. Until now, even though he was grovelling in the dirt, he was probably telling himself things like: after all, I am the son of a rich man, I am somebody. (I remember a *New Yorker* short story in which a tramp told a housewife: "I was somebody once.") He has that perverse snobbery that enables you to persist in consoling yourself with the thought that you're better than somebody, no matter how low you happen to have fallen, just because of your birthright or your original social status. But now it suddenly hits him that his aristocratic roots don't count for anything. When it comes to comfort—one of the most basic human needs—the servants have it way over him.

His first concern is his belly, his comfort. I think this is awfully important. He isn't concerned about abstract moral values. Neither is God, it would appear. He simply wants us to be happy and comfortable in our father's house. He wants us to lead the *good* life, a life that is fulfilling, satisfying, everything fine that a human life can be. That's the issue.

So the son smartens up and says he'll go back. But then he thinks: how is the father going to see me? It occurs to the son that he has blown it, that the father may be very angry and resent him, that the father may not be much inclined to take him back. No matter, he says, I'll acknowledge what I've done and just hope he'll let me work there.

Now here's one of the most serious problems of the story, for me: "I have sinned against heaven and thee." How did he sin against the father? To me, it's not all that obvious. Let's not fall into the old Jansenistic knee-jerk guilt: we're all terrible sinners, so you may as well throw the book at me, regardless of the fact that what I've done may have been as trifling as eating meat on Friday or seeing a restricted movie. What is his great sin, then? Wasn't he entitled to the property? Yes, so he can't be accused of stealing or wasting the father's property, as the brother claims. (Mind you, I'm not attempting to look into the question of whether or not the father could legally hand it over to the son before the father died. Maybe the whole operation was sort of shady; it may not have been in keeping with the commandment, "Honour your father and mother . . . .")*

Anyway, we look in vain if we try to zero in on some specific infraction that constitutes the sin. The business about the prostitutes is irrelevant. You can't link the sin to the sixth commandment; it's the jealous brother who invents that slur. Drunkenness, debauchery? I don't think any of them is the point.

The point of the sin, I think, is that he came very near to ruining himself, to losing his life, to actually dying. He could have been living a happy life in keeping with his blessings, but he let himself descend into misery and squalor. This is a sin against heaven—that is, against the life of God in him. This is not what any person is created for; this is not what human life is supposed to be about. He had been, presumably, a beautiful, fine person (with perhaps a touch of recklessness). Now he's made a mockery of the beauty of God's creation. And that's a great *heartache* to the father. The son

---

* Another thing strikes me: no mother is mentioned. It distresses me a little that Jesus could be so chauvinistic about the whole story. Yet, I can accept it because I think the story is very different from the father's point of view than it would be from the mother's. After all, the property was the father's business, I presume, according to the law. And the whole point of the story is the father's attitude. The struggle between the brothers, with the father caught in the middle, is very different from what it would be if you introduced a mother's point of view.

has wasted the gift of life that the father gave him. There's the sin. It has nothing to do with losing money or fornication (in themselves).

So it would appear that there are two aspects to the sin against the father: 1. The son has cut himself off from the father, refused the father's love. (No point getting into Freudian stuff about how he needed to reject his father—we all do, but in the end, there is still love, communication and all that.) 2. He has become, has let himself become, a sorrow to anybody who cares about him; his life is a mockery of what human life should be.

And yet I don't see it as all that culpable. Sure, he made mistakes, but there's no indication that he's an evil fellow. Far from it. He's just impulsive, irresponsible. There's no indication that he wants to hurt anybody, least of all his father. The son is just reckless. But he suddenly realizes that he has hurt his father. This is what saves him. The realization came to him when he actually pictured himself on the threshold; then he imagined the father's face; then he realized that he'd done his father a really big injury. So he admits clearly and up-front: Yes, I am a sinner, I did what I did and it's too bad. There isn't a lot of breast-beating and self-hatred and self-recrimination. He doesn't waste any time with that; he just gets up and goes.

Now we've arrived at the essence of the story. The crucial point. All this about how he sinned is helpful as a background, but it isn't the main message. The point of the story is the father's joyful welcome, the reconciliation. The nature of the sin is irrelevant to him. The important thing is: my son is back, he's alive! Overwhelmed with joy, the father runs to meet the son. This running shows how fully the father enters into the liberating experience of forgiveness. One tends to picture the father sitting there totting up the injuries and magnanimously cancelling out all the debt. Even though the scenario doesn't play that way, we hang onto that notion as a kind of sub-text. We imagine that the father would graciously put down the heavy burden of the son's wrongs, but that it would always be there in some dark corner, ready to be brought back to light, to reproach the son with if ever he should step out of line again. But no, no such thing. There is no burden, no weight. The father runs free. The wrongs suddenly no longer exist.

On Sunday the preacher mentioned that, since the father saw the son a long way off, he must have been watching for the son. This is a good point and I was glad to hear him make it. I think I first heard it about twenty years ago, perhaps from Father X. I am reminded of our hike with a group of strangers about four years ago. Michael (he was about eight years old) forged ahead with a man who claimed to know the way. When we came to the finishing point, there was no sign of Michael. He had disappeared with the strange man. We stood around wondering what to do. After several minutes, we spotted a kid, about half a mile away, trudging down the path towards us. What joy when, recognizing the logo on his soccer shirt, I knew it was Michael! (He was tired but otherwise unscathed; it just turned out that his companion hadn't known the way as well as he thought.) Someone commented on my good eyesight in being able to decipher the logo. It wasn't so much eyesight as a loving concern, a sixth sense, that enabled me to know him and his shirt a long way off, as the prodigal son's father did.

Once in a while I've heard people admit that they feel a sneaking sympathy with the older brother; his gripe strikes a responsive chord with some people who feel their lifelong faithfulness has been underappreciated in the flush of enthusiasm over the conversion of certain prodigals. Now I was going to say that I don't have any patience with these people. But I can be patient with them. I understand where they're coming from. Still, their attitude makes me sad, in that it shows how the Gospel has been distorted. As if life were a question of sitting there totting up rights and wrongs and seeing what your score is! That is not the point at all. The point is: you're alive or not. That's all. It's as simple as that. Either you are living in God's house, enjoying the good life, or you aren't. The father's delirious delight shows that this is all that matters.

Think of a parent losing a child: the worst thing that could happen, it seems to me. You would give anything to have the child alive again. Nothing else seems to matter. For instance—my recurring dream of my sister's being alive again. It turns out that she has simply been far away in a distant country. There was something disreputable about her adventure, but she is back now. Such a marvellous feeling. I'm also thinking of the L.'s, who lost an infant by drowning. Surely not a day goes by when they wouldn't give anything to have that child alive again. They must think of him often, if not constantly. They must dream of him frequently. Thank God, they have another son.

So all that matters is that we are alive and well and that we have each other. The little "sins" or "transgressions" are unimportant in the overall picture. It's not important that the son did this or that naughty thing. What's important is that he was lost, cut off, in darkness. But he came back—that's what mattered. Life and love are the important things. What a ringing testimony to the fact that Jesus stands for all that is best in human life! His message is not about some pharisaical moral code, but about the importance of living well and loving each other.

If you ask me, the older son doesn't have a legitimate complaint at all. He's abundantly blessed with his father's good food and comfortable house, but he thinks what's important is that he has obeyed orders. Not realizing that he has been showered with blessings, he isn't the least bit thankful for them. He thinks he has earned it all. Unaware of the tremendous giftedness of his life, he can't know what it is to be fully alive. He is spiritually dead. So he doesn't appreciate what it means for his brother to come back to life. The older brother is so deadened by scrupulous self-righteousness that he can't recognize joy when it's staring him in the face.

The fact that it was the younger brother's own fault that he ended up miserable is irrelevant. If your child died in a car accident but you could have the child back again, would it matter to you whether or not the accident was the child's fault? You wouldn't care less. When somebody comes back to life, you don't start splitting hairs over moral issues. People who do, like the elder son and the people who identify with him, haven't the faintest notion of what is really important: that life is a gift, that we are lucky and very blessed to have it.

That is the message of the Gospel, and especially of this passage, for me. No wonder I get sad when people who have supposedly been raised on the Gospel and have given all their lives to the following of their religion, can end up so badly missing the essence of it. They turn it into a case of rights and wrongs, adding up scores, judging and assigning blame. But the Gospel is about joy, life, praise, celebration.*

---

* The other night our group was reflecting on this parable and a couple of people said things that really struck me. D. said that the point of the whole story is *relationships*—that is, being with the father or not being with him. The father says to the elder son, "You are always with me . . . ." It's not about possessions, luxuries, and all that, even though he does add, almost as a throwaway line, as if to emphasize how little importance such things have, "All I have is yours."

On the other hand, L. pointed out how beautiful the father's statement to the elder son is. The father is a reconciler. He is not judging the elder son any more than the younger son. He understands the elder son's problem and the father is being much more compassionate and non-judgmental to the elder son than I am in the foregoing meditation!

6

Prayer

It surprised me, on pulling together the items for this section, to discover that there were so few dealing specifically with the subject of prayer. And yet, every one of the notes in my journals is an outcome of prayer and an extension of it. Maybe that is one of the major points of these writings: that all of life is a prayer, depending on how you look on it.

Lately I am being more honest about my moods towards God. One night I was very worked up about all the hassles at home and the office. I felt very angry at God for giving me such a difficult life to lead. Next day, I refused to get up to pray. I could not have prayed; I was too hostile to God. It seemed legitimate to feel this mood and live through it. A few days later, during Michael's soccer game, the sun was streaming across the green grass of the park, warming me. I began to feel again that it was good to be alive. I could feel my love of God coming back. The point is that the whole episode, including the anger and the refusal to talk to God, felt like valid aspects of a real, loving relationship.

•

This morning while meditating, I was aware mainly of the fact that my life lately has been a tumult of voices and activity. Yet, it felt slightly irksome to be required to break through this busy-ness, to find quiet time, to sit down and beg God to speak to me. But then I thought of it in the opposite way. Instead of my begging God to speak, it's God who's dying to speak. If I don't give God the chance, I'm the loser. Can you imagine anyone saying they didn't have time to hear their lover express his/her love? God is there all the time trying to say it and I have to create the opportunity for it to happen.

•

Most of the prayer period was restless and unfocused. The still point came only in the last few minutes. But running in the back of my mind for the whole period was the question: Do I trust God to speak to me in my imagination? Ultimately, God did!

After prayer, I was standing by the kitchen window. It was a dull, cold day, but the beauty of the morning glory on the garage really hit me. At first I didn't really notice it, but gradually it struck me as marvellous: a delicate, silky trumpet of white, with unimaginably subtle variations on pink, blue and purple. If I had seen a photo of it in a book, I would not have believed we could have anything so beautiful on our property. Here was a piece of extraordinary beauty sitting right here under my nose and it was only by stillness, by listening for the prompting of the Spirit, that I was able to notice it and get so much pleasure from it.

•

One afternoon, I went to pray in a sheltered nook in the rocks at Georgian Bay. I took off my clothes and lay exposed to the sun on a bed of ferns and moss. I prayed: "Here I am Lord, see me as I am, a man for better or worse, love me as I am, know me, acknowledge me, accept me." It seemed an odd thing to do but

I came away with the feeling that it was a healing experience at a deep level. It seemed to be a case of getting in touch with, or exposing, certain basic facts of my physical nature—the level at which I live simply as an animal creature without all the acquired attitudes, the poses, the masks and the roles, whose authenticity is never quite clear to me.

●

The other day while praying, I noticed something about my style of prayer. It's like making a stew. At the bottom, providing the heat and energy for the process is God's love. This is the flame, the burner on the stove which burns steadily throughout. Lately this flame is kept fuelled by the Jesus prayer repeated over and over. Sometimes I'm very aware of the flame and I concentrate on how beautiful it is. Sometimes, I just feel its warmth.

Meanwhile the stew that is me bubbles away. Occasionally, something special comes to the surface, or I'm aware of some unique aroma—say my pleasure in my kids or Jane, or my satisfaction with my work in general, or my appreciation of our group meetings. Other things come along to be added to the stew—memories of a delightful evening with somebody, worry about some business at hand, trouble with a kid, a problem with work, the recollection of an especially delicious cake. These are the incidentals that crop up every day. I toss them into the stew one by one as they come up. And it keeps bubbling away.

Sometimes I'm more aware of the ingredients being tossed into the stew; sometimes I'm more aware of the flame of God's love keeping it going. But both elements are there all the time. This I think expresses the hybrid quality of my prayer: part contemplative meditation and part gossipy chit-chat with God.

The upshot of it? *Awareness*, I guess. Awareness of God's presence in my life in every way. In the details as well as the fundamentals. Awareness of how God is inextricably bound up in my life. And, in the simmering process, there comes about a kind of self-acceptance: "This is what I am, Lord; this is what you have made of me today." So this brings a kind of peace and calm.

●

Yesterday on a walk through the vineyards I came to one of the stone sheds—a dilapidated one, small and very low. Its roof had gaping holes, there was no door, and inside were pieces of abandoned machinery and junk. I sat on the ground in front of it, with my back against it. My eyes were about level with the tops of the grapevines, so I couldn't look across the valley but had to look at the ground. Something fat and brown moved. I thought it was a mouse. Then I realized that it was a bird. There were lots of them hopping in the furrows. The field was full of them but, because of their protective colouring, you didn't see them unless you looked carefully. As they didn't notice me sitting still, they came very close. Another type of bird, sitting on a wire stretched between the vines, was pale greenish-grey with stripes on its chest. Eventually all the birds took fright and flew away *en masse*.

Loudly buzzing flies constantly zoomed past my head, in and out of the hut, but I didn't mind them much. Then honey bees came along, foraging in those white flowers (a bit like miniature phlox) that are everywhere. I plucked one and noticed it had a very beautiful, sweet but subtle scent. When the bees wanted to get at the flowers around my exposed ankles, however, I decided to move on.

While sitting there, I had fallen into prayer for a bit. The beauty of the Jesus prayer is that, once you've got used to it, you don't have to "say" anything. You can just *be*. Perfectly still. You don't even have to think anything, because the attitude of the Jesus prayer sums up everything there is to think or say about yourself and God. So you can "be still and know" that God is looking at you. There were only a few seconds of this stillness—not ecstasy or anything like that—just a sort of *stopping* in God's presence. It felt like getting in touch with the basis of my existence. Is this what's meant when they say that the best prayer occurs when you're not conscious of praying? Maybe this attitude can be carried over into ordinary daily events when you're busy with this and that, but somehow, without being aware of it, praying all the time.

•

Here's an example of how healing in prayer works. This morning I was very angry about a situation that had cropped up. When I sat down in this furious state to pray, I thought: Lord, I have had so much hassle, so much stress, that I just can't take another problem. And the loving answer came: "Right, you have had a lot of bother—the long train trip, your heavy cold, poor sleep, and all that. You surely don't need another problem. So relinquish this new one. Let it not be a problem." And gradually I began to feel myself letting go of the anxiety. I began to feel more peaceful. In fact, the thing that had been bothering me began to be a kind of focus of peace, a symbol of a kind of stillness of soul, a waiting, a darkness, not asking, demanding or seeking.

•

I haven't been praying much the last few days. Too troubled in spirit to sit and be calm, to let God's voice in. I'm just saying to God: you have to be with me, bear with me each step of the way; that will be my prayer, knowing that you are with me at all times. It will be an unconscious prayer.

•

Hadn't intended to meditate this morning. Felt very grumpy after the long sleep-in and the fuss over our visitors. But I decided on a short walk. Went up behind the chateau, then along the path to the west.

Found a place by two large rocks that provided good support for sitting, standing, kneeling. Enjoyed the bird songs, especially one with a rapid bubbling, cluttering and clucking, then a long trill. I prayed mostly just the prayer of Nature—listening to the birds, drinking in the green glow of the oak leaves, looking at the pink holly-hock-type flower with its fuzzy golden centre, hearing the buzz of the flies and bees, noticing the play of shadows. Not praying anything very specific. Just thanking God for being alive and breathing (and catching a bit of a scent despite an incipient cold).

Near the end of the prayer-like period, I was thinking about the memorial card for our old friend which bore the quotation: "This is all God asks of you: act justly, love tenderly, walk humbly with your God" (Micah 6:8). *Walk humbly with your God.* That expresses so much: friendship, a kind of solidarity, yet a love that lets God be God, that is content just to be human. *Your God*: that is, God within you, committed to you. *Humbly* . . . I love the idea of humility. It takes an enormous weight off: I am what I am before God. All the rest—the illusions, conceits, vanities, expectations (of self and others), criticisms—don't matter. I used to think of humility as an obsequious, smarmy, rather distasteful kind of grovelling. That's not it at all. I now see it as a liberation from all that is false in me. I see humility (if I had it) as the key that would unlock me from the tangle of my deceits, allowing me to soar freely in the clear air.

•

I have been thinking of that morning many years ago when I was standing in the garden around six-thirty in the morning, waiting for a ride back to the summer camp where I was working. It must have been August. I was looking at the dew in the garden, the spider webs, the structure and strength of them. What struck me most was the marvellous variety of the colours of the zinnias—infinitely subtle variations of pinks, purples, reds, yellows. That was when I fell in love with zinnias. Today I was thinking: these moments of great pleasure in life are moments of prayer even if you don't know it. That moment in the garden as a teenager was deep, unconscious prayer. I was feeling the father/mother inside loving life into me.

These instances of taking such pleasure in life, in a contemplative mood, are very important. At other times that pleasure will seem far away. You will find yourself groping in vain for the feeling of the life-giving love—which is not to say that it isn't there, just that you should rejoice in it when you do feel it. And you should not be ashamed that the prayer does not seem especially theological or "thought-out." It is just a simple human pleasure, a moment shared with God within you, like the child on its parent's lap (Psalm 131).

•

One of the reasons I find the recent busy-ness so overwhelming is that I am simultaneously leading a contemplative life within. I am thinking about what is happening. I need time to reflect and write. So my energy is drawn in two directions. Maybe that's why I can't put out constantly in the busy way that a lot of people do. Not that they don't also reflect and pray, to some extent, but they don't need to do it as much as I do. They seem to be content to do it on the run, as it were. Maybe their thoughts are deep enough in their own way to satisfy their needs. It could be that they don't have to articulate their prayer life as much as I do. Maybe, in ways more subtle than mine, they get right down to the meaning of things. At any rate, today it was interesting to see that my prayer could at this time be a simple, wordless acceptance of all that's going on, a recognition of God's life in this interaction among loving people. Apart from that, my prayer right now offers no insight or intellectual gratification.

•

My prayer lately is mostly lying on the floor with my hands out, saying: Yes, Lord, I accept all that is going on, all this hectic inter-relating with people, the irritations as well as the pleasures, the effort to accommodate the individual needs of each person. I'm accepting that this interaction is very important. This is the substance of life. This form of prayer that amounts to the acceptance of my busy-ness is surprisingly satisfying. I just lie there and rest, letting the many thoughts and memories of the day wander at random through my mind. I am too tired to do otherwise.

•

Last night, while I was hopping into bed to read, it suddenly occurred to me how content I was: we have nice warm rooms (I've been putting the heaters up higher—why not be comfortable?); we had good food at supper, a little wine; Michael was tired and satisfied after a birthday party; I was particularly pleased with the way my painting had gone in the afternoon; Madeleine was happy about her one-hour visit on her own to the neighbours and she had many anecdotes about their animals . . . .

So, realizing how content I was, I spent a quiet moment in bed before reading. My thoughts tended to flit away very quickly because of fatigue. But I felt that it is good to be alive, to have family. And that amounted to prayer. I think that is what they mean when they say the best prayer comes when you're not aware of it. Your heart is singing a song to God who is within you; it's spontaneous and genuine. You're not getting down on your knees and offering pretentious formulae to the God Up There. You are communicating with the life-sustaining Spirit inside you, even if you don't recognize the process as prayer.

•

Prayer this morning was mainly an awareness of mental turbulence. So many ideas, projects. One minute

I'm happy and looking forward to many things; next minute I'm depressed and unbearably tired. In the Iris Murdoch book I'm reading, there are ideas on every page that make me want to stop and think. It's overwhelming. It all goes by too fast. I tried to think of Psalm 131. It was hard to arrive at the peace and stillness described in the Psalm, the simplicity and openness to the present moment. Contrary to the spirit of the Psalm, I like to hang onto my "lofty" ideas. I'm always reaching for theories, great formulations—because they give me comfort and security; they reassure me. There's the thing! That's why it's hard to let go of the craving for them. What's more, that sort of intellectualizing has been admired in the society I belong to. So I'm always pushing myself to come up with new insights, new formulations, that will "guide" me. But the only formulation I need is: be content, grateful, open to the Lord, see what happens.

7

Religion

*While all the previous sections deal with spiritual-
ity, this section focuses more specifically on what is
generally thought of as the expression or manifes-
tation of religion in our society. For me it has been
a long search to find out what is true religion as
opposed to the chimeras that are often mistaken for
the real thing. To make these thoughts seem a little
more coherent, I have grouped them in three cate-
gories.*

A.   Piety, concepts of holiness and dedication.
Some false trails in my search for them.

It was very hot in church on Sunday. Suddenly I
had a flash of the old image of myself sitting alone in a
church, listening to the birds at the windows, commun-
ing with God in a life of quiet, monastic holiness. The
religious feeling was very real and powerful. So I'm
thinking: why is it that I haven't been able to live
always with that religious sense? Well, it seems to be
one of the mysteries of my life, that as much as that kind
of holiness seems to appeal to me on a deep level, it isn't

the life God wants for me. Besides, there's a tremendous amount of self-absorption and narcissism involved in that longing. In that monastic image of myself, all that matters is to polish my perfection. There isn't much engagement with other people except as a duty consequent upon my holiness.

•

On the subway, I saw a nun in a funky black coat with a fur collar. The poor look of the coat reminded me of how I used to think I could embrace poverty as a monk or priest. I thought I could give up everything as long as I was assured of getting God in return. But it wasn't God I wanted. It was security, comfort, feeling good about myself, the illusion that I possessed God. Now it seems to me more likely that we meet God, not in "poverties" that we take on voluntarily, but in life as it happens to us, mostly through other people.

•

This has become increasingly clear: what the seminary gave me and what I loved so much about it was order, discipline, structure, predictability, security—and thus a relative peace and serenity. That's all fine and enjoyable if it soothes your spirit. My great mistake has been in identifying such structure with holiness, with being close to God. What it is much closer to is self-satisfaction.

•

Standing in the dark church for a moment, looking at the glowing red vigil light, I was reminded of how much that scene used to "inspire" me with devout impressions: the austerity, the silence, the feeling of being close to God, alone with God. There's nothing wrong with that feeling, unless it makes you feel isolated from people, special, better, "holier"—in other words, if it makes you think you can only find God in the solitary confinement of your own broken heart and not in communion with others. You have to know in the depths of your being that you are loved by God, that you meet God there, but it should be a kind of love that confirms your communion with other people, that emphasizes your ordinariness, your common humanity, not your special "holiness".

•

While driving the dusty road to the dump, I got the old feeling of holiness that used to come over me while walking in the country after intense prayer and meditation. It was a feeling of being filled with God, heavenly light shining on me, a feeling that I had embarked on a great moral struggle that lifted me above the common herd. At those moments, I used to feel that I was breaking into the pure, rarefied air of the High Road. Now it hits me with a kind of pang to realize that that feeling is lost and seems likely never to come again.

And in its place? When I think of being close to God now, experiences that come to mind are more communal, more outward-directed. For instance, there was that night at the supper table when B. was talking quietly about the history of her birth. She often dreams that her father comes back to her, that he's a prince or some such hero, that he's driving a "limo" and that she forgives him everything. As she spoke of these deep feelings, my heart went out to her. It was a real experience of the compassion of Christ reaching out and connecting me to another person. Any irritability I had been feeling on account of her was swept away.

•

Meditating this morning on the rich young man (Mark 10), especially about "leaving all and following Christ." This notion used to prompt very strong yearnings in me. Like the feeling of almost delirious joy during the first weeks in the seminary, when I felt cut off from everything, embarked on life with Jesus only. Is this just sentimental, romantic nonsense? Well, a lot of it is. But at the core of it is the expression of a very fundamental and true longing: you want Jesus to bring out all the good in you. Fair enough. The mistake is in thinking you can leave behind the grime of your complicated personality. It takes years of living to discover that you don't escape your basic nature. At least, I don't. Religious education and spiritual guidance were much inclined to make me think that I could escape to a realm of perfection, of sublimation, at which point I would have left behind my mucky self. Not so!

What would it mean, then, to drop all and follow him truly? I think in the first place you have to look at the context of the encounter with the rich young man. Jesus was inviting a contemporary in first-century Palestine to become one of his disciples and help spread the Kingdom. Jesus had a big job to do and he needed lots of people to help; they couldn't be tied down by other concerns. (Mind you, he told others to go back to their daily business.)

Could that sense of giving up all else for Jesus apply to joining a religious order? It might. It depends on how you define Jesus' work. I don't think that building up the power and might of the institutional church—with massive schools, hospitals and the like—is necessarily Jesus' work. On the other hand, it isn't inherently evil either. It's part of the fabric of human life. There's nothing wrong with a woman being a hospital administrator and calling herself a nun if that's where her inclinations and talents lie. She may be expressing very well the life of God within her. But her situation doesn't necessarily or even likely make her a better witness to Christ, a better example of God living through people, than the teacher in the public school or the ditch-digger.

Then how does the labourer, the professional, the homemaker follow Christ? I think it amounts to letting yourself be led by the Spirit gradually. It's not a once-and-for-all decision by which you leave everything behind—only someone with the outlook of an adoles-

cent could think that. Bit by bit, each day, you learn to
listen for God's voice, to let yourself be stretched and
forced to grow in ways that you wouldn't if you clung
to your "possessions," that is, your hardened notions of
what you are and what you want to be, of what you
must have for your contentment and comfort. Letting
go of these, you eventually become more loving to
other people. You're helping in ever more ways (perhaps never conspicuously) to make God's love present
among people.*

The point is that giving up house, family, possessions, taking on celibacy and all that, don't of themselves have anything to do with following Christ. The
professed religious is having his meals provided, a roof
over his head. Why does this lifestyle make him "closer
to God" than the man who worries about mortgage
payments, about putting food on the table? Food and
shelter are not alien to God's concerns. God cares about
such things and wants to see people well-clothed and
fed. So I think it's likely that the person who is struggling with these concerns is discovering the life of God
just as authentically as the religious who is administer-
ing some huge, powerful institution.

•

[After talking to a couple of priests working at a
retreat house:] While I felt some envy of their opportunity to discuss with people the things of the heart, I felt
a little distanced from the institutional aspect of the
priests' lives. This awareness of the disagreeable aspect

---

*   These thoughts were prompted by reading an article in which a
young priest said something like, "It is now ten years since I gave up all to
follow Christ." I wanted to cry out: "You fool! What makes you think you
gave up all? Don't you hang on to your interests and your obsessions, to
your love of power and control, to the gratification of seeing your pious
thoughts published? People wait on you, serve you meals. You don't have to
earn your living with the same sense of responsibility that most people do.
How can you claim to have given up *all* for Christ?" (Admittedly, a
somewhat intemperate reaction to the young priest!)

of institutional religious life is quite a change in me. Previously, I liked the institutional side of religious life, at least for stretches of time. Now, not only do I see it as uncomfortable and relatively inhuman, but, on a deeper level, I'm moving away from the feeling that God is to be found necessarily or most likely in these "religious" settings. I'm becoming much more excited about the way in which Christ finds us and speaks to us in every aspect of our ordinary lives.

•

While touring the Franciscan monastery, I was inspired by the words of Francis emblazoned everywhere: how love is the be-all and the end-all, how kindness to the brother is so important, and so on. Moved by the spirit of Francis, I thought, why don't I give myself to God completely? I have so often wanted to. Maybe I really can after all. What's holding me back? Complete dedication to God has always been something that I want. This is what's deepest and truest in me.

If I have wanted to give myself to God and have tried so often, how come it hasn't worked out? How do I find myself wanting to try again? Well, it seems you just can't live at that level of idealism. You can make the great gesture of throwing yourself on love, committing yourself to love—but, in due course, ordinary life intervenes with all its ups and downs and you have to keep adjusting in order to survive. You can barely keep your head above water, let alone throw yourself into great exploits of love. At least, that's the way it is *for me*.

And what about this: am I not leading a life of love? I'm married and I'm raising kids. It's all based on love. In this context, most of all, I experience God's love. So what does it matter if I don't feel ecstatic about it? Does that mean I'm any less dedicated? What difference would it make if I stuck a label on myself like "Frère Patrick of the Holy Family" or something like that, and wore funny clothes and tried to make myself distinctive by living in an institution (or some bizarre hovel) and drew attention to myself by keeping to an unusual routine? Would any of that mean that my life was any more fully dedicated to love?

Look at the old religious who become crotchety and depressed despite their great youthful enthusiasm and their promise to live totally for love. Are they any more dedicated than I? Clearly, the great ideals usually bog down in complicated human affairs. Does that mean the ideals are futile, illusory? I guess not. We need them. But it seems to be given to very few people to live them in an exemplary way—or, let's say, in the way that I used to envision them being lived. Just the occasional Francis of Assisi or Thérèse of Lisieux.

All of this is my very belated appreciation of the place of ideals in our lives. They have to be balanced by a realistic sense of how life can be lived, as opposed to the illusions that a lot of people, for reasons I do not know, tried to foist on me.

•

Something became clear to me the other day. While reading XYZ (the newsletter of a small religious group), I was feeling the old confusion. On the one hand, the articles about living for love and love alone, the sense of intense dedication, made me want to live that way. Yet I was simultaneously aware that my many attempts to follow up that yearning haven't worked out. Is it all bullshit? It suddenly struck me: the longing is true and beautiful. Where it begins to seem phoney—turning into pietism and religiosity—is when those people make it seem that anyone could live out those nice, fine feelings all the time. Maybe some can. Not me. I can't live my life at that pitch of fervour all the time. I simply have to be able to come home and shut the door, so to speak, and say, "OK, I don't feel any zeal right now. I have to be my grumpy, natural self for a while."

•

After one of my really bad temper outbursts, I was thinking about an article in which a young member of a religious community was going on and on about the fact that she longs for Jesus only, that all life is pain and emptiness apart from him. I was thinking: what nauseating, neurotic stuff masquerading as religion. Here's a woman who's congenitally incapable of adjusting to normal life and getting along with other human beings in an ordinary way, but she translates this disorder into some kind of mystical yearning!

Suddenly, in the context of thinking about my temper outbursts, I began to sense some very important differences between my situation and the attitude expressed by the writer of the article. I may be just as neurotic as she is in some ways, but my temper tantrums ensure that I'm not putting on a pious act. I can't pretend to any of this "mystical" rot because my temper tantrums won't let me get away with such a charade. They always bring me down to earth. You could say that my temper tantrums are my touchstone with reality. (Perhaps I shouldn't be referring to the tantrums, which can perhaps be avoided, but to my *struggle* with bad temper. This, I suppose, isn't avoidable.)

Another touchstone with reality for me is my relationships. These relationships make me intensely angry at times, but they are real. I'm in touch with real people to whom I am irrevocably committed and I can't shirk the relationships no matter how much I might try to escape to a pie-in-the-sky religiosity. I can't run off to some hermitage and pretend that "Jesus is all" because I am stuck in a situation where I have to struggle mightily with the human realities.

•

At the church door, G. was giving me her motive for all her church work: "Either you believe in God or you don't. If there is no God, then the little we do for him is ridiculous. If there is a God, then we can never do enough . . . ." It seemed like an ironclad, irrefutable dictum. She was obviously very pleased with it. Her attitude reminded me of my meditation during the summer after my first year in the seminary: after reading the New Testament, especially Paul, I wondered how believers could let themselves be mediocre and lukewarm. I came to the conviction that we must all strive for the heights.

But life taught me that there was something screwy about that conviction. It seems to me there must also be something wrong with G.'s dictum. It's too pat. If it is true, why don't people live by it? The problem with the dictum is that it is not true to the way God relates to us. God does not oblige us to knock ourselves out cleaning rectories, arranging flowers for altars, rushing around to meetings and liturgies.* God is among us in everything good that we do. There is the divine in every genuine human encounter. There is no reason to suppose we should whip ourselves into a back-breaking frenzy of "Church service" to please God. How does it serve God? Why would God want it? Is it to placate God? Or is it to try to make sure that religion dominates our lives? I think that G.'s statement shows the scrupulous, guilt-ridden, anxious background that she is operating from, even if she would appear to be functioning on a more positive level.

•

After the monastery visit, as we were eating in the hotel, there was an elderly mother in the dining room with her mentally handicapped adult son. I had to remind our kids not to stare at him. I wondered how hard it was for the mother to endure his noises and

---

*   I don't mean to imply that one should never exert oneself in the service of the Church (which, after all, merely means the service of each other), that one need not do anything to express one's religious instincts outwardly. Church activity is fitting and good: the outward expression of our connection through each other to God. What I'm criticizing is the "we-can-never-do-enough" mentality. It seems to me that this is neurotic and obsessive, although it often passes for real religious devotion.

gestures. Did she come down for supper early to avoid as many other guests as possible? I was struck by the holiness inherent in his limitations—the complete dependence on God, the complete lack of prestige. His is a life where love is all that matters.

Then it occurred to me: is not my life—with my handicaps, my limitations, my frustrations, my failures—close to God in the same sense as the mentally handicapped man's life, *closer* even than if I were a good monk, living a serene life of virtue, perhaps very content with myself? The answer came with a resounding YES. In this life, I am discovering my dependence on the love of God and of others, in a way that I can't imagine discovering as a monk. Not that there is any such thing as a good monk who is self-satisfied, of course. The mere fact that I could picture myself as a monk, serene, content, "above the fray," is proof that my inclination towards being a monk is totally misdirected, skewed. So, what I am trying to say is that in family life I am losing myself, accepting my poverty, my "death"—or, am at least on the way to accepting them—in ways that seem very well-suited to who I am. The life God has intended for you, the life where you find yourself, is certainly the one in which you best find God; that's where you get rid of illusions about yourself and accept your poverty.

•

This morning while reading *Poverty of Spirit*, I came to the passage where Metz talks about how one can miss the moment when one has the chance to put one's life together, to make the right decisions and to move on. I was reminded of the many times I have had "conversions" and have started again on a renewed commitment to the Gospel. The Vanier retreat came to mind. The point that interested me was this: why have I so often had these wonderful religious experiences but end up back at square one, where I seem to have no religion, where my religious feelings profit me nothing, where I have to start over? How is it that, after all these years, I seem to have gained no security in virtue? How is it that when I am full of religious love, at times like these retreats, I feel I am going to scale the heights, I am going to be very good from now on . . . yet it doesn't end up that way?

Well, the answer came very simply and clearly while reading: God wants me to muddle through in this very imperfect way because then I'll have to depend on the Spirit, not on my own virtue. If things had gone swimmingly from that first conversion, I would be so full of self-satisfaction that true religious development would be impossible. I was not meant to be a religious "star." That would be totally destructive of any true growth in loving openness to others and in the true spirit of humility. If I were not constantly worn down by this irritable nature of mine, I would become terribly full of pride.

This "answer" seems terribly obvious now, to the point of being banal. But it struck me with tremendous force and it seemed that I internalized it for the first time. What is quite clear now is that my being full of good religious feeling is not all that important. Moments of intense fervour are valid stages in human growth; they inspire you and provide the enthusiasm you need at turning points. In the long run, what matters more is trust in God throughout the humdrum, monotonous days, trust in spite of irritability and discouragement with yourself. All that really matters is a willingness to keep going, to let God do it, even when you're not pleased with your "progress."

•

On our trip to the Abbey de Senanque, I was wondering if I would feel the old pull towards peace and purity that monasteries usually exert on me. We descended the long hillside road, so narrow that you had to pull into a lay-by to let another car pass. The abbey, a squat but splendid Romanesque building, floated above a field of lavender haze in the hot, still valley. Inside the reception area there was a modern, churchy feeling, with piped-in Gregorian chant and large posters on the wall recounting the history of the abbey. Jane liked the squarish church with the rough stone, freshly cleaned, the vault very high, very austere, and the simple modern altar. There was a heavy incense smell.

On the way out, we noticed a monk giving a spiel to a group of fat, tired tourists. The monk was thin, middle-aged, with a scraggly beard and glasses. The white of his habit was soiled, especially at the hem. It was hard for me to catch much of what he said, but his manner conveyed an impression of nervousness combined with self-importance. He was shy yet sanctimonious. Pointing to a diagram of the church, he said, "The church is built this way because this is the shape of the cross on which Christ died." People looked at him with mute respect.

I wanted to blurt out: "Who are you, buddy, to lecture us about God and holiness? Go get yourself some kids and you'll learn a lot about life that you don't know now." His way of life is fine if that's where he finds meaning for himself, but I strongly resent the implication that he has any monopoly on holiness, on the understanding of life, love, and God. I reject his stereotyped veneer of holiness that forces these honest ordinary people into a misplaced awe. Probably any one of them could tell him lots about the true meaning of life if they knew how to put into words their experiences and instincts.

•

At our meeting the other night, L. was relating how she has been reading St. Benedict and how he says all that is asked of us is "simple fidelity." This suddenly means so much to her. She used to long for the bolt of lightning that would knock her off her horse and give meaning to her life. It strikes me that our great longing for the dramatic religious event is really just escapist. It may not even be a fundamentally religious drive. Maybe it's just a longing to have our vanity satisfied. It's as if we're saying that it's impossible for God to be present to us here and now in our very ordinary selves. I suppose a lot of this escapist fantasizing stems from the distorted religious education which instilled the hatred of self and the idolatry of heroism. And yet, there is a sense in which the longing is fundamentally and authentically religious in origin. It stems from our deepest yearning for union with God. But our own self-hatred and the education which reinforces it pervert that longing into the dream of glorious escape from ordinariness.

B.   This section deals largely with the pursuit of virtue.

One of the most startling insights at P.'s funeral: she was by no means a perfect person, but *that doesn't matter at all*. This seems obvious; yet, for me, it's a discovery. She had faith, although not the kind to boast about; it was part of the package of her many colourful virtues and flaws. In the end, it didn't matter a hoot that she wasn't perfect. This realization on my part is very different from my thinking throughout my formative years and most of my adult life so far—that you must always strive for a kind of perfection. Indeed, it seemed to me that my adult models were virtually perfect. The purpose of life, as demonstrated by them, was to keep trying to develop a finely polished character with no rough edges.

Why did I feel this way? When I look around, it seems to me that lots of good people would never think of trying to be perfect. For example, T.: she strives not to hurt people and to be decent and fair. She is very loving to most people. But it would never occur to her to present to the world the image of a woman of perfectly balanced virtues. She just accepts that when she's mad, she's mad. When she's impatient, she's impatient.

Likewise when she's sad, melancholy or depressed. As for my comrades back in the seminary, I think most of them (the sane ones, that is) would scoff at the idea of trying to be perfect, although they did try to be good people.

Yet, the official line was that we should strive for perfection. At least, that is what I heard. A "lukewarm" believer such as P. used to be an embarrassment to me. I had the fire in my belly to strive for the heights. I suspect the change in my point of view has a lot to do with psychotherapy and with coming to the awareness that my striving for perfect holiness had a lot to do with self-hatred, with the desire to escape what seemed my sinful self, the refusal to accept and love myself as God made me.

●

The other night, in a discussion with Jane about some problem or other, I said, "God gave each of us a very limited range of virtues, and if we try to stretch that range we're only fooling ourselves." It just popped out of me. Yet it seemed very true. How could I have hit on something important so suddenly, after leading my life for a long time according to a very different understanding? Next morning, I considered again, more coolly, whether or not what I'd said really could be true. It seems to me that it is. If we are not very charitable, not very patient, not very tolerant or whatever, we have to admit it, without kidding ourselves. We have to recognize that we aren't likely ever to exemplify those virtues very well.* But this does not mean that we do not, on occasion, decide to act more generously, more charitably or more tolerantly than is our natural inclina-

---

* What I was trying to point out here was that it is good to recognize one's natural limits in terms of specific virtues. However, on further reflection, I think it should be said that in the Christian life, one hopes to be led very gradually by the Spirit to a fuller appreciation of, and respect for, one's own life and that of others. This process could be described as growth in the virtues of patience, charity, and so on.

tion. In other words, we can, and should, in some cases, step outside our usual behaviour patterns and act according to the standards of a particular virtue that we don't really possess. For me, the important thing is to be careful not to lay claim to the virtue on the basis of that one instance.

•

While one would expect to become a better person over time, I find myself even more lacking in virtue, goodwill, and loving intentions as time goes by. It keeps happening: all of a sudden I'm up against the wall and I feel nothing but hate, anger and frustration. All my fine religious notions, my well-polished image of myself as the good, spiritual person, avail me nothing. For example, I get into a sticky situation at work, or into a conversation with X that turns disagreeable. It is only with great difficulty, and not with any consistency, that the situation is resolved with an appearance of good grace on my part. I suppose that this is when the saving grace of Jesus Christ becomes operative in a specific situation. I am enabled to do the right thing regardless of how I feel.

•

So much exasperation yesterday. Mostly about the children's school problems. Also recurring resentment about parish affairs. Tension over technology problems, not to mention chronic stress over our visitors. My thought while falling asleep: when all your faith seems to amount to nothing, when you seem to have no religious resources to fall back on, when you're filled with hate (it seems), anger, resentment, and you have no good, pious, wholesome thoughts or feelings to buck you up—that's when faith means something. I'd always thought that one would be resilient, that one would have lots of spiritual resources to fall back on— like D.'s style: always undaunted, always ready with an ideal to cover every situation, never defeated or discouraged, never down and out. I pictured faith like a tank of gas that you filled up in the good times so that you could draw on it when you suddenly needed a quick burst of spiritual energy in an emergency. The way it turns out, however, is that one day I'm full of faith, the next day—nothing. Perhaps this emptiness, this bottoming out, is an essential aspect of my life. It doesn't seem out of keeping with the Psalms and the Bible. It only seems out of keeping with a 1950s-style triumphal Catholicism, as I experienced it growing up.

•

In contrast to the zealots with their euphoric life, here's what mine is like. I wake up early, usually after a short night, and, while meditating, I'm in love with life and with the whole human race. Then I launch out into the real world and by eleven a.m. I'm tired, disgruntled and angry. I rest at noon. Then the same cycle in the afternoon. By tea-time I'm fed up and irritable. It occurred to me that the (shall we say) theological (as opposed to biochemical or psychological) reason for these slumps, these bad moods, is to keep me humble. By that I don't mean dejected, dispirited or thinking badly of myself.* I speak of humility here in the true sense of the word: in touch with the truth, fully aware of it, accepting it—fully cognizant of my limitations. If I carried on day after day in the exalted mood of the early morning, I'd be thinking I was the fourth person of the Blessed Trinity: totally loving, serene, happy, and all that. But the slumps constantly remind me that I need God's strength to get me through.

•

---

* Obviously, I do feel dejected and rotten about myself while in these slumps. But that's not humility. That's just emotion. If I could face the situation with humility, that is, with acceptance of my limitations, then there probably wouldn't be so much negative emotion.

An elderly priest writes in his memoirs about how his spiritual director taught him to be meek, kind and self-effacing, never to raise his voice in anger, and so on. I find myself asking: what has this to do with Jesus? It's ludicrous to think of that manly, dynamic, first-century Palestinian Jew being so self-absorbed that he would worry about whether or not he raised his voice. That old *Imitation of Christ* spirituality is, in effect, a denial of the wholeness of being human. Isn't there a very strong measure of narcissism in such spirituality: this preening oneself, always insisting that one must show superior restraint and kindness far surpassing that of ordinary humanity?

Of course, it is necessary to acquire some self-restraint and kindness in order not to impose oneself on others, in order to allow others to live freely. But I think that, at best, these virtues probably have only a cautionary value. They act as brakes or safety devices. They aren't the essence of holiness at all.

What, then, is the essence of holiness? If you ask me, it's acceptance of God in others and oneself, rejoicing in creation and being thankful for life—like the child content in the parents' house.

I was going to say that it made me sad to think of the old priest having tried to live his life according to a misconstrued sense of holiness. But, on reflection, I have to admit that his pursuit of such virtue was probably no worse than basing one's life on any of the thousands of other theories we find for ourselves. Somehow God's will gets worked out through our groping for what we can't see clearly. And isn't it possible, after all, that the old priest's "meekness" is an expression of the very fundamental holiness of not wanting to impose his will on others?

•

Lately, I have been prey to terribly black moods. Problems arise with the kids; there are conflicts between me and Jane. I'm helplessly plunged into the pit. A couple of awful attacks of bad temper in the past week. On one occasion in particular I felt no love, no faith, no kindness—just ugliness, evil. I felt like a lump of shit. None of my religious training seemed the least bit relevant or helpful. It all seemed a charade. My supposed "fine feelings" towards other people and God were completely gone. I felt like a hateful bastard—driven to the bottom of despair by problems that totally overwhelmed me, situations for which all my religious education left me totally unprepared. I had never imagined myself ending up so totally lacking in any faith or love, so utterly bereft of things that had seemed to make me what I am.

In spite of the awfulness of it, maybe it's a kind of cleansing. It feels good to be made aware that I am perfectly capable of not being a fine person, of abandoning all my lofty principles.

•

More and more it occurs to me that my place religiously is at the back of the temple with the publican. There is an awful lot of the Christian message that I don't live up to and I don't even intend to. Not to mention large parts of it that I don't understand. Yet, having met Jesus Christ, I feel he is the answer. For me, he is the light in a world of darkness and confusion. So, I want somehow to tag along in his camp despite my not particularly distinguished status therein.

C.   In this section I ponder various manifestations of what is usually thought of as Religion with a capital "R".

I'm struck by how people invent religion for themselves. They fashion religious experiences and insights according to their own needs. For instance, the lawyer in C. P. Snow's *Brothers and Strangers* undergoes an earth-shattering conversion and thenceforth makes religion his be-all and end-all. Closer to home, there are people like W. and Z. who claim to have had similar experiences. Such people need a dramatic thrust like this in their lives to give them the sense that all is worthwhile, that they have a reason for going on, that all is not lost in boredom or despair or pessimism. They think that this dramatic intervention comes from God on high, that they've been zapped by some sort of bolt from heaven; whereas it's all really just their inner needs speaking to them. Which is just fine. I'm not implying that their zeal is false, that their faith is illusory. God does work within us in the context of our own needs. Their crying need for direction and meaning is truly God speaking within them—in a different way from the way God within me speaks to my needs.

There are people whose inner needs cry out for a rigid universal moral law, for an authoritative, hierarchical structure of religion. Such things make them feel that there is order and sense and goodness in life. Perhaps they need this kind of reassurance because of temperament, or the theology they have been handed, or their upbringing (the atmosphere of the home, the attitudes to right and wrong, to matters of control and subjugation of others). These factors lead to formulations of a God who responds to all these notions. (Sometimes, however, the formulation of an authoritative, totalitarian God can be a reaction against a lack of authority and discipline in early years; the image of God isn't necessarily an exact projection of the one received from parents and elders.)

The problem is that these people often can't see that their formulations of religion are an expression of the kind of God they themselves would *like* and *need* and that this is no justification for imposing it on the rest of humanity. Of course, it is part of their belief, part of their need, that religion be totalitarian and all-obliging, that it *must* be imposed on everyone. This is where I part company with them, because this leads to fanaticism, totalitarianism and tyranny in the name of God— some of the worst evils in human history. It would be OK if they could have their own little totalitarian, authoritative societies within their own circles—and leave the rest of us "heathens" outside. But they'd not likely ever be satisfied with that. They'd always feel that they should *try* to convert the rest of us. And I suppose that's all right. Wanting to convince someone, to win others over to your side, is a natural human inclination. I have no problem with that as long as we remain *free* to not be converted—with no penalties other than those consequent upon the ordinary unpleasantness of having to disagree with someone.

•

On the subway, I ran into N. who was in a glum mood because his wife's car had broken down and he had to bring the kids to school. He started telling me about his recent visit to a friend who is a Benedictine monk. N. told me how happy the monks are, how they love God totally, how his monk friend had been married, with kids, but had his marriage annulled.

I fumed about that for quite a while. Not so much the issue of annulment, but the mind-set of the 1950s Catholic family man who is awed by these celibates who are "totally" given to God. The assumption is that God cannot possibly be totally present in the lesser, mundane lives of us sexually active husbands and fathers with our "worldly" concerns. An escapist, monastic Catholicism promotes alienation from self, a denial of humanity. It makes me angry because the elitism of it has done much harm to individuals; it has warped their growth and it has denied the world the awareness of Jesus living among us.

•

Why can't I accept N.'s constant recourse to officialdom? Well, because I see it as destructive to true human growth. I'm angry about the lost opportunities for individuals to truly discover God in themselves. Nevertheless, on the personal level, I can accept that if N. feels that his views help put *him* in touch with God, then that's fine; his ideas, although repellent to me, are

just part of the complex fabric of humanity. My resentment has to do with the threat of his views being
imposed on everyone.

•

About the encounter with the recently "converted" religious zealots. It's very disconcerting when
someone I like turns face and tells me he's a changed
man. The worst of it, though, is the *guilt* that these zealots lay on you. (Whether or not they consciously intend
this is a good question.) They inevitably make you feel
that if you don't follow their example, you're lost. In
every encounter with them, there is this subtle pressure. Wrestling with the anguish these people have
caused me, I seem to have discovered that deep inside
me there appears to be rooted the old notion that there
can really be only *one* way and that you're screwed if
you don't get with it. So maybe the way of the zealots is
the one way? This thought produces all kinds of guilty
speculation: maybe all my personal, emotional troubles
would be resolved (as they claim theirs have been) if
only I'd give in and "accept" their way; so I'm to blame
for my trouble if I don't capitulate? Are we, then, to
blame for our family troubles because we're too stubborn to turn our lives over "totally" to the Lord, as they
claim to have done? Hence, the terrible, prolonged
argument between Jane and me about our family problems when we got home from the upsetting evening
with the zealots.

•

The zealots' attitude is not only a denial of the
freedom of religion but it's an abdication of intelligence
and humanity. In other words, an outright denial of
what the humanity of Jesus means. Jesus' humanity, in
my understanding, is meant to show us that we are not
supposed to have the assurance of arrant gods, as these
zealots seem to have. I think we're meant as humans to
experience doubt, confusion and pain.

The reason the zealots' enthusiasm is particularly distressing is that, for me, it has been a long, hard struggle to achieve a kind of sanity about religion, an integration of religion, good emotional health and daily life. So it is a terrible wrench to hear them suggesting that maybe, if I just capitulated, there really would be an end to all my problems and an ecstasy and fulfilment such as I used to hope for and actually did try to achieve by different religious means at different times.

After all my fuss and confusion about these people, maybe the issue simply comes down to what Jane says: "I know an awful lot of very good people who don't sound a bit like those two." How very true! That's not to deny the zealots their measure of goodness. But our model of goodness derives from a very different kind of people.

•

About recent reports of appearances of the Blessed Virgin—the insidious consequences of the message (as I hear it) repel me: you're a bunch of evil creatures and this world is going to hell in a handcart, you must all begin to hate yourselves, torture yourselves and suffer. *If* you're extremely lucky and *if* the capricious, mean, vindictive God relents, you *might* be saved.

This is the opposite of Jesus' message, as I understand it. He confirmed that the world is good, that it is good to be human, to be of such mixed nature as we are. He came to show us that God is in us and in the world. He came to affirm, not to condemn. What an enormous difference this perception makes in my world view—not just my feelings about myself but about my neighbours, the business world, entertainment, and so on. Catholicism boasts a strong tradition of the life-denying negativism espoused by the Vision adherents. But, at a certain stage in my life, it simply wouldn't work for me any more. It was too destructive. I had to turn from it and face the light without looking back.

None of this is to deny evil in the world. Jesus mentioned it often. There's plenty of it around—the destruction of the environment, the ruin of so many lives by the greediness of the drug barons, the stockpiling of armaments while millions of people starve. The difference between my outlook and that of the Visionists is: what is your starting point—self-loathing or love of self and the world? The Visionists start with the assumption that humanity is rotten, that it's going to be a Herculean struggle to pull ourselves up out of our human condition and achieve some measure of godliness, thereby convincing the haughty God-Up-There to notice us.

•

People have turned religion pretty much into the opposite of what Jesus meant by it. What his life and death are all about is that it is glorious to be fleshy, ordinary human beings. In the past, I thought the goodness of being human involved a much-sanitized humanity, a striving for perfection that amounted to "angelism". That's a serious perversion of Jesus' message. His life proclaimed that it is fine to be the weak, moody, fallible creatures that we are—this is divinity in us, divine life expressing itself in human form. And he was the example par excellence of that combination because he was so fully human and down to earth—to the point of being poor and suffering a horrible death. His example was of no use to us if he was just masquerading as a human, condescending to pretend to be one of us. If his divine life were not fully and authentically incorporated in humanness, then, in aspiring to share in his life, we would miss the beauty of being truly human and we'd be doomed to failure. I think that his life, his loving, his death, his speech, his eating, sleeping, and all the rest of it, show that there is divinity in us just as we are—thinking animals. This is the finest life for us.

•

Some people are talking about bringing back the Friday fast. They're calling for clearer rules and more of them, almost a complete return to the old days of the Catholicism marked primarily by penances. It seems to me that they are saying: "We tried, in the spirit of Vatican II, to be more loving, more free, less rule-bound, we tried to take a positive approach to Lent rather than a negative, penitential one—but it didn't work, we found ourselves adrift, we found we weren't more loving, more tolerant towards our neighbour, we found that we didn't and couldn't become better people. So, please, give us some rules for God's sake so that we will know now where we stand. We will have the comfort and assurance of knowing that we are good because we keep these rules. We won't have to be bothered anymore with this tiresome business of having to be open, compassionate and understanding to others."

•

In spite of my impatience fairly bursting out of the previous note, I am trying to take a broader view of religious practices. There are many disparate approaches to religion in this parish—Madame L. with her fussing over the sick, her First Fridays, her trying to run the liturgy like a frustrated priest; there is Monsieur W.'s pharisaism, his holier-than-thou attitude; Madame L.'s youthful enthusiasm; Madame T.'s feisty defensiveness. I see all this variety as God working in and through people. It's the community trying to express its faith as best it can. Formerly, I felt that there was one right road, one high road, the only route to God, the approved one, and that everyone must be made to get on that track—the one chosen by me. The fundamental difference in my outlook now is the recognition of God in all people, as opposed to God on high towards whom we must struggle to haul ourselves up. We all express God in our unique ways. It's a belief and trust in humanity, finally.

•

How very much my idea of God is changing! And yet, even to speak of an "idea" gives the wrong impression—as if it were a philosophical or theological theory to be worked out step by step. My sense of God is more like an awareness, an opening up to a greater and greater appreciation of what is there all the time, what has always surrounded us and always will. Still, the "ideas," the images and notions that you pick up at the various stages of your life probably remain with you in some form or another. You can probably never really change them or get rid of them. What I'm sensing is the way in which all these ideas and notions merge to create something so much greater and more all-encompassing than previously imagined.

My sense of God can now absorb many different interpretations and expressions of the divine. For instance, let's look at the time when my concept of God seemed much more limited—the time in the seminary. My faith then consisted largely of adherence to truths handed down to me by teachers, parents and superiors. Loyalty to barely grasped doctrines, ludicrous as it seems in one respect, was nevertheless one legitimate aspect of the expression of God in our lives: it is a good thing to be loyal to the beliefs of your parents, to try to live up to them, to use those principles to make of yourself a fine young man.* But now I see the adherence to those stated positions as just a small part of the overall picture. I am astounded more and more by how truly catholic, in the sense of universal and all-embracing, my awareness of God is becoming. It would appear to be a genuine recognition of God because it leads to more compassion, tolerance, peace, and openness to others.

•

---

* The adherence to given beliefs was not totally superficial. The handed-down tenets had been tested, within my limited experience, and found to be valuable in terms of making sense of my life.

What if somebody said, "Chuck all this religious palaver and just get on with living. Your 'religious trip' seems like a self-indulgent hobby that gets in the way of real life." Well, if somebody takes that view, fine. If they want to chuck all these religious practices of mine and simply try to live a good life, fine. I'm all for that. The goal, after all, is a life well-lived. That's all that matters. So I can chuck the constant preoccupation with religion, the "religiosity" if you want to call it that, because the essence, what's important, remains.*

•

I become more and more appalled with the world of conspicuously religious people, whether they be professionals or hobbyists in religion. Such involvement isn't the mark of true goodness or holiness in God's eyes (if I may speak for God!). It is not those who run around saying "Lord, Lord" who are in touch with the Kingdom. It is not necessarily the Catherine Dohertys or the John Mains who truly live and know the Gospel, even though they pay lip service to it constantly. (I'm not trying to judge the inner lives of these people—I'm only saying that the outer show, all the "Lord-Lording" counts for almost nothing. At heart, they may or may not be true Gospel people.)

It may be the job of some people to talk up Gospel just as it is the job of some people to pick up garbage and of others to teach school; having religion as your job (this applies to those for whom it is an avocation too) does not make you a better person or closer to God even though you are perhaps an expert on the theory. This may seem obvious, but I don't think enough attention is paid to the distinction. In my upbringing, an automatic assumption of goodness was granted to anyone associated with religion. While it may be my calling, to some extent, to preach and write about the

---

* The purpose of the religious practices is to help me lead a good life. Some people may not need that help.

Gospel, that does not mean that I am more worthy than anyone else. Of course, I am good—but not because it is religion I peddle. Doing whatever I am meant to do, be it talking about choreography or the stock market, would make me good.

•

What about people who appear to be following a Christian life (showing such qualities as love of family, loyalty, honesty, and such) even though they cannot believe in Jesus? In effect, they have heard the Gospel message in their hearts and are following it, although they don't identify with established religion. I think their problem with Christianity is that Christians have used the Gospel as a battering ram; they have set it up in opposition to science and common sense. They have declared a war in which the God of the Bible is pitted against the God of Normalcy. Sometimes the biblical miracles are used as the ultimate squelch. The religious gloat: "See, our God beat your god!" This, I think, is why many good non-believers cannot accept the Gospel message. They have not been shown, by example as well as explanation, that the message is primarily about conversion of heart. *Anybody*, smart or stupid, scientist, poet or whoever, can accept that.

•

Today I saw two men standing on the sidewalk talking. They seemed nice people, especially the hearty old man who was waving his walking stick as he spoke animatedly. He looked like the naturally good person, one who wouldn't need a lot of religious input in his life. He didn't look as if he would ever spend much time pondering religious niceties.

I wondered: could it be that much of Jesus' message was directed at those of us who love to muck about in religion, who have a penchant for "religious" life? He was warning us that it's a dangerous occupation, that it can be self-deceiving, illusory and totally destructive of the true life of the Spirit. People who have the life of the Spirit in them without a lot of religiosity don't need these warnings.

This helps to explain something that has long puzzled me: how is it that only religious people bother much about Jesus' message? He came for the whole world, not just for the devout. Could it be that many good people have heard his message in their hearts? That's why they don't need a lot of obsessive pulling and poking at his teaching.

I'm not saying that anybody is totally good, that people who aren't religious are necessarily better than people who are religious, or that anybody is totally bad. Everybody needs Jesus' message; we all need to clean up our act, to call on his help to make us more loving, more tolerant, and so on. What I'm saying is that a lot of people can be pretty good without a lot of fuss about religion. It is those of us who are prone to self-deceiving religious trips who need to study more closely Jesus' message. He said lots to set us straight—if we could hear him clearly.

PRINTED BY THE WORKERS OF
IMPRIMERIE D'ÉDITION MARQUIS
IN NOVEMBER 1994
MONTMAGNY (QUÉBEC)